I JUST GOT FIRED.
NOW WHAT?

I JUST GOT FIRED.
NOW WHAT?

A GUIDE TO FINANCIAL SURVIVAL
AFTER LOSING YOUR JOB

DAVID L. BLAYDES,
MS, CFP®, AIF®, RFC

GREENLEAF
BOOK GROUP PRESS

Published by Greenleaf Book Group Press
Austin, Texas
www.gbgpress.com

Distributed by Greenleaf Book Group

For ordering information or special discounts for bulk purchases, please contact Greenleaf Book Group at PO Box 91869, Austin, TX 78709, 512.891.6100.

Design and composition by Greenleaf Book Group and Kim Lance
Cover design by Greenleaf Book Group and Kim Lance
Cover sign image: Thinkstock/iStock Collection/ayzek
Cover businessman image: Thinkstock/iStock Collection/Pinkypills

Cataloging-in-Publication data is available.

Print ISBN: 978-1-62634-278-1

eBook ISBN: 978-1-62634-279-8

Part of the Tree Neutral® program, which offsets the number of trees consumed in the production and printing of this book by taking proactive steps, such as planting trees in direct proportion to the number of trees used: www.treeneutral.com

TreeNeutral

Printed in the United States of America on acid-free paper

18 19 20 21 22   10 9 8 7 6 5 4 3 2 1

First Edition

*Susan, I've been married to you for over thirty years
and love you more today than ever.*

*Bridgette, Lauren, Megan, and JD, I've accumulated
several designations, MS, CFP®, RFC®, AIF®,
but the one that means the most to me is DAD.*

*Just as I have dedicated my life to you,
I wish to dedicate this book to each of you.*

*While I have provided the means,
you have provided the meaning.*

CONTENTS

PREFACE ix

ACKNOWLEDGMENTS xv

INTRODUCTION 1

CHAPTER 1

STEERING CLEAR OF BUMPS IN THE ROAD:

10 Financial Potholes to Avoid 5

CHAPTER 2

KEEPING A FULL TANK:

Where to Go for Cash When You Need It Most **25**

CHAPTER 3

GETTING A FINANCIAL TUNE-UP:

How to Trim Your Expenses **51**

CHAPTER 4

EXTENDING THE WARRANTY ON YOUR 401(K):

How to Protect Your Largest Investment **75**

CHAPTER 5

SETTING YOUR FINANCIAL GPS:

The 91.5% Asset Allocation Factor **111**

CHAPTER 6

KEEPING RIGHT:

How to Review Your Portfolio **127**

CHAPTER 7

TAKING THE WHEEL:

How to Create a Sound Financial Plan **137**

CHAPTER 8

REACHING THE END OF THE ROAD:

Converting Investments to Income **153**

CHAPTER 9

GETTING A GOOD MECHANIC:

Tips for Finding the Best Financial Coach **161**

AFTERWORD **177**

APPENDIX

PERSONAL BLUEPRINTING **179**

ABOUT THE AUTHOR **223**

PREFACE

FRIDAY, MARCH 16, 1979, was the date I got fired. I say "fired" even though I know that is not a politically correct term today, but in 1979, you didn't get "downsized," you got fired. I had started my financial planning career right out of college and was hired by a major financial planning firm in Chicago after six months of rigorous interviewing and testing. For me, the brokerage firm route didn't fit. I didn't want to learn how to sell an investment; I wanted to learn the technical aspects of financial planning, even though I realized it would require years of training. I also wanted to recommend and do only what was in my client's best interest, not what was in the best interest of a brokerage firm. However, I knew I needed to learn the business before I could consider making a change. I had school loans to pay off, so I considered the job a learning resource for my future and an opportunity to pay off some school debt.

Once hired, I was "that guy" who got in at 7:00 a.m., had breakfast, lunch, and dinner at my desk, and caught the 11:00 p.m. train home every night, even though everyone else, including management, worked 8:00 to 5:00. The train commute to and from the office provided another hour of study time each way. I happily helped the other brokers and found it reinforced my own learning.

The owners loved my work ethic, and, when they observed me helping others, they put me into a management-training program, which was normally reserved for people who had over three years of tenure. I looked forward to Saturdays, because I was the only one in the office, which meant ten to twelve hours of uninterrupted study and work time. I came to work one day with a temperature of 104 degrees and had to be driven home. I had burning desire, was hungry for knowledge, and was full of energy. (Thirty years later, that hasn't changed.) I broke all the training records, completed the first six-month training module in three months, and was on the fast track. And then I got the call on March 16, 1979, at 3:15 p.m. My father had just been in an accident, and his arm had been severed. Because the accident occurred many miles from a hospital, it was uncertain if he would be alive when I got home. The doctors told me my dad was headed to surgery to complete an amputation and they would try to save him, but I needed to get there as fast as I could. He had lost a lot of blood. I ran to Phil, my manager, quickly told him the story, and said I had to go home. I was in Chicago, and my parents were a hundred miles away, so it wasn't like I had requested an extensive leave to fly somewhere. My manager didn't say he was sorry for my bad news, good luck, or even "I hope your dad makes it."

Instead, he said, "It's less than two hours from quitting time. Wait till 5:00 to leave."

I responded, "He could be dead by then," and I left.

Dad lost his arm but survived. The following Monday, I returned to work. I was called into my manager's office. I was expecting him to ask how my dad was doing. Instead, he fired me for leaving work early. There was no acknowledgment that for months I had worked ninety-six hours per week when everyone else worked forty. But right away, I knew I did not get fired for those few minutes. I got fired because my manager's boss had been giving him a hard time, because one of his guys worked twice as hard as he did. When the company put me in the management pool so early, I became a threat to his position, and I bruised his ego when I left work before he said I could. Yet, fired is fired. I'll never forget his words; never forget that feeling of anger after working so hard. I felt rejection and feared that I wouldn't be able to make my car or apartment payments. I remember the feeling of cleaning out my desk, the walk out of the office, the train home. I kept trying to figure out what I was going to say to my family and friends.

Over thirty years later, I'm blessed to be able to say that only the death of my and my wife's parents were worse days. I share this story only to make this point: If you are reading this book because you have been terminated, I get it. I understand every feeling, fear, and emotion. I've been there.

After I was fired, I decided to go into business for myself so that an insecure manager could never hurt me again. It was one of the best decisions of my life and one that I have never, not once, regretted. Looking back, I can see that getting fired was the best thing that could have happened to me at the time. Not only did it give me the motivation to open my own business, but it also provided me with the fear of failure combined with a burning desire to succeed in a business where I could help others, and these feelings fueled success beyond my expectations. I've had the pleasure of being asked to make multiple TV and radio appearances, receiving awards from our leading industry newspaper, *Investment News*, and gracing the cover of our leading industry magazine, *Financial Planning*. I was ultimately able to fulfill my desire to help people with true financial planning instead of just trying to sell them something. I secured my certified financial planner (CFP®) designation and a master's degree in financial planning to make sure I was proficient in the technical areas of my profession. Then, I earned my accredited investment fiduciary (AIF®) designation and have followed its mandate to only recommend what's in my client's best interest, something that I am adamant about.

I was able to put myself in this position, to have the ability to only recommend what's in my client's best interest, by becoming independent, free of any brokerage firms' conflicts of interest. More importantly, as I married my wife, Susan, and we had four children, Bridgette, Lauren, Megan, and JD, having my own financial firm provided me flexibility, so I was able to keep my family my first priority. I was able to coach football, baseball, basketball, and soccer while all the other dads struggled just to make the weekend games. Later in life, working for myself allowed me the resources to send all four of my children to the college of their choice, Purdue University, even though it meant sixteen years of out-of-state tuition. I am able to work with my family, in a career I love, a career that allows me to help others every day. All of this because an old boss said those dreadful words, "You are fired." Today, I would look him in the eye and say, "Thank you, Phil!"

Like me, you could also be on the verge of a positive change that you're not able to foresee at this time. So together let's ensure you don't make any financial mistakes during this transitional time that could cost you later. Steadying yourself in the best possible financial position is a crucial first component to embarking on a successful journey. You may not be able to control what your past employer did, but you can control the financial impact of it.

> You may not be able to control what your past employer did, but you can control the financial impact of it.

You don't need to take this trip alone. I've specialized in working with terminated employees since 1992, when my friend Scott Robinson had a talk with me over lunch at TGI Fridays in Naperville, Illinois. Scott drew out a business plan on the back of a napkin describing how I could help those going through a job transition in the outplacement firm he was a partner at, and I have specialized in job transition financial coaching ever since. Good talk, Scott.

Whether it be from this book, our website (www.rpiplan.com), or one of our financial coaches, we can help you navigate through this difficult time.

ACKNOWLEDGMENTS

MY DEEPEST APPRECIATION TO my father, who taught me that a handshake should mean more than a contract; my mother, who taught me the joy derived from helping others; and my brother, who showed me that you can reach the top of your field without stepping on anyone if you take each step upward with integrity.

To my wife of thirty years, for being my best friend and unselfishly supporting me as I built the firm, I am forever grateful. In the first few years of our marriage I worked eighteen hours a day, and she never complained.

To the best four kids a dad has ever had: Bridgette, Lauren, Megan, and JD. Thank you for inspiring me every day to be the best dad possible while you were growing up, and now that you're grown, hopefully, one of your best friends. To my sons-in-law, Anthony and Jared, thank you for showing me that the perfect family can get even better with the right additions. Speaking of additions, thank you Bridgette & Anthony for giving me the best birthday present I have ever received with the birth of our first grandchild, Brooke Nicole, on February 21, 2016.

And although it may sound odd, thank you to my clients. When I started a family, you told me how fast life goes and ordered me home in the evenings and on weekends. You have mentored me on how to handle the emotions of walking a daughter down the aisle and handing her off to another man. You convinced me that there was vibrant life left in the empty nest as I drove my last child to college. By sharing stories and pictures of your own grandchildren with me, you have taught me to look forward to having my own. Many clients that have passed taught me that if you live your life right, your influence continues even after you are gone. I know, because I am now working with their children.

During the first half of my career, those I worked with were twice my age, so they had already been where I was going. I taught you how to reach financial independence, but it was you who taught me how fast life goes, the importance of always keeping family first, and that helping you would allow me to have a career with so much meaningful purpose. I have learned more from you than you have from me.

INTRODUCTION

ON THE OUTSIDE YOU may be sporting a great front with
a smile, but inside you are wondering . . . where should I take
money from first? If I sell some non-IRA assets, am I going to
have to pay taxes on the gain? How can I reduce my cash flow?
Should I take money out of my 401(k)? If I'm under the age of
59½, is there any way to avoid the 10% penalty? Even if I don't
withdraw from my 401(k), what should I do with it? What's the
difference between a direct distribution and a direct rollover?
How do I make sure I don't make a mistake that costs me thousands of dollars in unnecessary taxes and penalties? What's the
best thing to do from a tax perspective? If this transition takes
longer than expected, am I going to be able to make my mortgage payments? Am I going to be able to keep my child in college? How can I make sure this short-term job change doesn't
derail my long-term financial goals?

Let me explain the reason behind the car and trip analogy.
I have found that when I start talking about financial issues
to someone, I often see their eyes glaze over, and I know I've
lost them. Reading about technical financial strategies is not as

interesting as reading a good novel by your favorite author. The road trip analogy was chosen to convert to terms that are more easily identifiable while symbolically tying your current journey into one of a road trip.

I know you have these questions because I have specialized in working with Fortune 500 company employees and out-placement firm candidates as soon as they are terminated from employment since 1992. Our firm has worked with thousands of individuals like you, and 99% of the time, people ask the same questions.

This book will answer those questions, as well as many others. It will show you where to go to first for cash flow and the income tax consequences of your options. Several techniques for reducing cash flow and taxes are given. The pros and cons of the four options you have with your 401(k) will be described, including what you can and cannot do, and should and should not do, with your retirement funds. If you need to take withdrawals from retirement funds before age 59½, a technique to avoid the 10% penalty will be given.

In addition to providing you with the technical details on how to make the best financial decisions during your period of transition, those we work with typically replace fear and anxiety with a feeling of reassurance and confidence.

You will also find the term Financial *Life* Plan throughout the book. I'm not just about the numbers. One of the first things I've always told my clients is, "*You* are my client, not your money."

I am just as concerned that my clients are living a life with meaningful purpose as I am that they can pay for it. This book focuses on what to do with the money and numbers. The Personal Blueprint in the appendix focuses on what to do with the person by focusing on five key areas: values, meaningful purpose, compelling vision, personal mission, and goals. The combination of the two produces a Financial *Life* Plan to help you achieve true wealth—what money can't buy and death cannot take away.

Bottom line: I want to give you some financial guidance and emotional peace of mind, so that you can focus on your job search. The pages that follow will do just that, so turn the page and let's get started!

CHAPTER 1

STEERING CLEAR OF BUMPS IN THE ROAD: 10 FINANCIAL POTHOLES TO AVOID

PLENTY OF PEOPLE HAVE ideas about how to endure a job loss. Some ideas are insightful, and others can seem off the mark (usually because the advice comes from folks who have never really experienced this difficult period). There are many pieces of wisdom I could offer you about what it means to weather a job transition, but I'm confident that this will hit home: At this moment, the situation you're experiencing probably feels like the scariest possible thing that could happen. I have specialized in outplacement Financial *Life* Planning for the past twenty-five years of my thirty-year career. Like you, having suddenly lost a job, I *get* what you're going through. This is not an easy time. Fortunately, there are strategies that will not only help you avoid costly short-term financial mistakes but will also *improve* your long-term financial outlook by

> **You will get through this.**

the time you get back to working again. Let me reassure you: You *will* get through this.

ENGINE TROUBLE

I know you're thinking, *David, I'm not worried about my long-term financial outlook; I'm worried about paying my bills this month.*

I understand and respect that—even though I don't want you to do anything now that will derail your long-term plans, I agree that the short term is exactly where your priorities should be. The best financial strategy you can use during your job transition actually addresses *both* of these concerns simultaneously. Think of your financial life just as you would a road trip. If our life journeys require us to keep our financial fuel gauge from getting too low, transitions like the one you're experiencing are like engine trouble.

Think about your job transition this way: You have encountered a problem with your car and need to pull over for a while. Once you have pulled over, you have two choices. Either you can make a quick fix that will help you get down the road until you stall again—something similar to repairing a radiator leak with duct tape—or you can talk to a certified mechanic. If you do the former, you'll certainly get by for a short while, but just like that radiator will start to leak fluid again, if you don't make the best choices with your money right now, you might wind up leaking cash or other financial assets unnecessarily down the road.

During my time working with countless individuals transitioning between jobs, I have found that people who forgo the quick fix in favor of talking to an expert are more successful in both the short and long term. Meeting with a specialist helps you make prudent decisions based on logic, experience, and knowledge rather than making decisions based on your fear of losing the lifestyle you've grown accustomed to. So let's figure out the best strategy to help you keep the bills at bay without sacrificing your financial future.

CHECK YOUR FUEL GAUGE

When most people are in a transitional period like the one you're in, after they have finished worrying about how they will tell their spouse, family, and friends the news, the next things they worry about are finances. Financial anxiety almost always starts with the same question: "Where should I go for cash?"

Next, people worry about how they can reduce their monthly bills to make life a little more affordable. When you don't know when your next paycheck is coming, these are natural concerns. Fortunately, job transition is usually temporary. You *will* get back to work eventually—or, if you're retiring, you will become comfortable in due time. In the short term, the best thing we can do is find the most effective and comfortable way to bridge this wage gap without destroying your chances for long-term financial independence.

Unfortunately, when faced with a drastically reduced cash flow, too many people fail to think about their financial decisions as they relate to their Financial *Life* Plan. A Financial *Life* Plan is more than just an investment portfolio. It is a roadmap that helps you get from where you are now to where you want to be when you're living your ideal life—financially, personally, and in terms of your career. It is not only a vehicle to help you make, invest, and maximize the money you will have both now and in retirement; it is a strategy that guides you toward living the life and working the job of your dreams. A Financial *Life* Plan is the ultimate balance between smart finances and living with meaningful purpose. I have included a Blueprinting Guide in the appendix of this book to help you create a Personal Life Plan and Financial *Life* Plan.

It's easy to forget about how your long-term financial outlook relates to your life both now and in the future, when you've lost a job or are transitioning into retirement. If you think about your Financial *Life* Plan as a gas gauge, then your goal (even while you're searching for your next job) is to keep that financial gas gauge as full as possible. Too many people find themselves drawn toward cash sources that hurt them financially. In the beginning of this book, I will help you avoid this critical mistake and potentially save you thousands of dollars in unnecessary taxes and penalties.

I understand that knowing where to go first for cash is important, and I promise that we're going to take some time and discuss how to get money when you need it. For now, keep in mind that not all cash sources are created equally—and you

 might be surprised to find that taking cash from certain places could actually cost you more money than it's worth. Before we get into all that, let's talk about a few potholes on your road to success that you will want to steer clear of during your time between jobs.

10 FINANCIAL POTHOLES TO AVOID

You're under a lot of stress right now—whether you're transitioning between jobs or into retirement. I get that. The paycheck you relied on is gone. The people who depend on you for that money are in danger of seeing their lifestyles change. Your future looks uncertain for perhaps the first time in a long time, or maybe even for the first time ever. I've seen many people in your shoes that start to panic about things like keeping their kids in college or paying their mortgage. A large part of what we do as a firm is help calm these situations before our clients make financial mistakes that stem from emotions. The good news is that, once we get a chance to discuss the best financial strategy and start to figure out where the money is going to come from, you will feel better about your situation. Job transition is difficult. Fortunately, it's not the end of the world. You will get an income again—and probably sooner than you might think. What we need to focus on in the interim is the best strategy for preventing your financial engine from breaking down while you search for that income.

Many people in your situation make the mistake of treating job loss like a complete engine failure. I understand why it seems that way. Your paychecks aren't coming anymore, so it probably feels like you're stuck. Well, I like to think about it another way. Your job loss doesn't mean that your engine has stopped running. Rather, it means that the little red check engine light on your dash has started blinking. If you've ever seen one of those little red lights, you know that it doesn't mean immediate disaster, but it does mean you need to start thinking seriously about what you're going to do to *avoid* disaster. It means that if you don't make the right decisions soon, you're going to wind up stranded on the side of the road with smoke billowing out from under your hood.

When your check engine light comes on, the best thing you can do is visit a certified mechanic. Such an expert is best equipped to help solve the problem before it develops into an engine-destroying situation. The same is true for your job loss. The car that is your Financial *Life* Plan is still running (even if it doesn't feel that way at the moment), but if you don't take action and visit a financial coach soon, your engine just might sputter out before you can find new work. I'll talk about how to find the right financial mechanic toward the end of the book.

If you're anything like me, the first thing you think when that check engine light comes on is, *Okay, what went wrong?*

The answer to this question can come from a multitude of

directions. We're talking about a complex engine here, after all. The same can be said for the complexities of your finances. Well, if facing a job loss is exactly like a check engine light coming on, then let's ask that same question as it relates to your finances. "What went wrong?" In my many years of experience working with those going through a job transition, I have found that "what went wrong" for most people falls into one of ten categories. These are the 10 financial potholes that you need to avoid:

10. EMOTIONS: Don't make decisions based on emotion.

Job transition can be an emotional time, and it's difficult to control emotions during emotional times. However, as you have probably learned from your own life experiences, decisions made out of emotion are usually the kinds of decisions you wind up regretting. The problem with following your emotions during your job transition is that poor decisions could cost you thousands of dollars in unnecessary taxes, penalties, and future compounding interest.

> Job transition can be an emotional time, and it's difficult to control emotions during emotional times.

Hit the Brakes

When the red check engine light comes on in your car, are you more likely to step on the gas or hit the brakes? Of course you're more likely to hit the brakes—and that's exactly what you should do with your financial decisions. Hit the brakes. Before you make any decisions about what to do with your money and where to find income during this transition, get a Financial *Life* Plan done. I'll show you an example of a plan, and how to get one, toward the end of the book. This way, during this difficult period, you can rest assured that all your financial decisions are the *right* ones

 because they are based on a logical plan instead of an emotional reaction. If you don't want to do a full plan, then at least hit the brakes and pull over long enough to consider all of your choices. We'll be discussing those choices later. In the meantime, hit the brakes, not the gas.

9. DEBT: Don't incur the wrong kind of debt.

Did you know that there's good debt and bad debt? As long as you don't buy and borrow above your means, your mortgage is an example of good debt. This is because it allows for a tax deduction. It's also kind of nice to have a roof over your head. As a bonus, a house is an especially good bit of debt at the time of this writing because, unlike the early '80s (when I bought my home), interest rates are at historic lows. I have seen individuals withdraw from their newly accessible 401(k) funds, at an income tax rate of 25% and an additional pre–age 59½ 10% penalty, to pay off their mortgage balance of 5%, which was really costing them 3.75% after their income tax deduction. Paying off a net 3.75% mortgage with funds that cost 35% to withdraw is a mistake no matter how "good" it might feel to pay it off, and this doesn't take into account how much these funds could have potentially grown to if they had not been withdrawn to pay off the house.

Credit cards are an example of bad debt. This is because the interest rates are typically somewhere in the neighborhood of five times that of mortgage rates. The interest is also not tax deductible. So the next time you're in a retail store and the cashier tells you that you

> If you don't control your debt, it will ultimately control you.

will receive a 10% discount if you apply for their store-branded credit card, you might try my favorite line in reply: "I'd rather pay you an extra 10% not to have another credit card!"

As you examine your debt situation during your job transition, remember this: If you don't control your debt, it will ultimately control you.

8. LIFE EXPECTANCY: We are living longer.

On a recent trip to Hallmark, I noticed the birthday card aisle had a section dedicated to people celebrating their one-hundredth birthdays. I can't recall ever seeing so many cards for that milestone before. If Hallmark didn't see a need for a one-hundred-year-birthday card, they wouldn't have a section for it. In fact, at the time of this writing, for an American couple currently sixty-five years old, there is a 50% chance that one will live to age ninety-two and a 25% chance that one will live to age ninety-seven.[1]

So the good news is that your life will probably be even

---

1   John Deppe and Angela Deppe, *It's Your Money! Simple Strategies to Maximize Your Social Security Income* (Rolling Meadows: Second City Books, 2012).

longer than the lives of the generations before you. As medicine continues to improve, life expectancies will only increase. You might very well receive a one hundredth birthday card of your own someday. (The tricky part will be remembering who sent it.) It is great to think that you might have many more years ahead of you than you may have anticipated. The bad news, however, is

> You don't want your money to run out before you do!

that the longer you live, the more money you will need. I know your golden years might still seem like a long way away, but if you fail to plan enough for a long life, this job loss won't be the most difficult period you will have to endure. That stress you feel today? You will be feeling it again when you're old, and unlike now, it might not be temporary. Don't make financial mistakes today that will hurt you in the future. You don't want your money to run out before you do!

7. SOCIAL SECURITY: It can work for or against you.
President Franklin D. Roosevelt signed the Social Security Act into law on August 14, 1935. Although the program was simple then, the changes to Social Security over the past eighty years have resulted in a lot of complexity. Social Security can work for or against you.

Some people think that Social Security is not nearly as financially stable as it once was—and even if it is, the program has seen changes that can affect all of us. For instance, if you earn too much before reaching your full retirement age, after retirement, you will see your benefits reduced by as much as 50%. Many think the threshold for the reduction is very high when it's very low. As of 2016, you start to lose a dollar for every dollar earned over just $15,720. Once you reach your full retirement age, there's no deduction for income, but you might have to pay taxes on your Social Security income. Imagine being penalized for working! Well, that's exactly what happens with Social Security if you don't plan properly.

If you're earning too much money, you might find yourself getting taxed on your Social Security. In 2016, if you're married and filing jointly and your adjusted gross income is $32,000, you pay tax on 50% of your Social Security. At $44,000 of Adjusted Gross Income (AGI), you pay tax on 85% of it. For single tax payers, you pay tax on 50% of your Social Security once your AGI reaches $25,000, and at $34,000, you pay tax on 85% of it. This might come as a surprise to you, because if you are anything like me, Social Security feels like a tax in and of itself while you are working. So to be taxed on something that felt like a tax to begin with, well, that is like having two check engine lights coming on at the same time.

If you are at an age where you can start your Social Security and you plan on searching for your next corporate gig, make sure you take what I just wrote into account before you run down to the Social Security office; I have seen as much as a $250,000 lifetime difference between picking the earliest option and waiting for the best option. Although it might seem like a distant concern right now, these insights are important to keep in mind as you take the time to establish or revise your Financial *Life* Plan, and here's why. If you don't properly take it into account when doing your plan, the plan can recommend an asset allocation with more risk than necessary as it's trying to make up for the income not properly stated from Social Security.

6. PENSIONS: A thing of the past.

My father worked for the same company his entire career. I remember every year at Christmas he would get his choice between a turkey or a ham. At his disability-forced retirement, they gave him a gold watch and a pension. These days, chances are you won't be getting a gold watch or a pension at retirement—you probably won't even get a turkey or a ham! This is because, over the past few decades, most companies decided that they wanted to take the burden of planning for your retirement off their own shoulders and place it squarely on yours. So they got rid of the pensions they used to pay for and gave you a 401(k) that you pay for. In fact, pension plans have decreased from 62% of companies offering them in 1983 to only 17% offering them as recently as 2010.[2] No lifetime pensions combined with longer life expectancies. Are you starting to see why it's critical not to make any wrong turns with your money during your period of transition now that could cost you later? Times are surely changing rapidly, and so we must make sure that your short-term and long-term investment strategies keep up.

---

2   Ibid.

Unfortunately, many common investment strategies are out-dated. I have met with clients that thought they would have company-sponsored pensions when in fact they would not. Others have been most troubled to learn that, after their job loss, they would no longer have access to the money they would have received in a pension if they had retired from the company that just let them go. It can be a devastating mistake to plan for that money, only to find out you are not utilizing the most prudent pension option or not even getting it at all.

5. POOR INVESTMENT CHOICES: Don't invest the way I drive.

Most people invest the same way I drive. Think about the last time you drove through traffic. Maybe there were two or three lanes on the road, and all of them seemed to be moving at different speeds. Well, if you're anything like me, the lane you're in is almost always the one moving the slowest. So what do I do? I move over to the lane that looks like it's moving the fastest. But what inevitably happens when I do that? Yep, my new lane slows down, and the one I just left starts moving faster. I don't know about you, but I've started memorizing the cars around me, so I can see how I'm doing. Usually, I don't do so well. The craziest part is that even though I know this happens almost every time, it doesn't prevent me from repeating the same behavior the next time I encounter traffic. My wife, Susan, tells me that it's because I have an inherent problem when it comes to driving: I'm a man!

This is exactly the way the majority of people invest. When you receive your 401(k) statement in January, you look over your returns from the previous year. You find one fund that did considerably better than the others. So what do you do? Just like changing lanes in traffic, you change investments and move to the one that appears to be moving faster, due to its higher return. Then, the following January, when you find that your new fund didn't perform as well as another one, you switch again. Before you know it, you've lost a lot of ground on the cars around you. I call this tendency *chasing returns*, and it has proven (time and time again) to be inferior to determining your needed rate of return with a Financial *Life* Plan and then creating a well-diversified portfolio to give you the best chance of achieving that rate of return without any more risk than necessary. In fact, chasing returns is such a poor strategy that it's actually *worse* than changing lanes of traffic—it's more like driving on the shoulder—dangerous! Guess when I see people doing this the most? Yep, during their job transition, as they roll their 401(k) into an IRA investment that had great performance the previous year.

4. UNNECESSARY TAXES AND PENALTIES: It's not what you make; it's what you keep.

> It's not what you make; it's what you keep.

It's not what you make; it's what you keep. When I think about taxes, I like to think about the best ways to minimize the effect taxes have on your life. There are a number of ways to avoid unnecessary taxes and penalties when looking for cash, and knowing these is crucial to staying on the correct road to short-term and long-term success. Incorrect financial decisions (especially during a job transition) can lead to the kinds of taxes and penalties that can be financially crippling. This period is difficult enough without these penalties.

This is an especially important point to remember during this time of your life, because the first place people turn to for fast cash following a job loss is their 401(k) or other qualified retirement plans. You do this because you think of your retirement funds as "your money," and as money that wasn't as available to you while you were working. So now that your employer no longer has control of your 401(k), you might make the mistake of viewing your retirement plans as free money.

As we'll discuss in chapter 2, this strategy—the strategy that most people in your situation turn to *first*—is actually the *last* place you should go to in search of cash. This is because funds withdrawn from your retirement plans are fully taxed. In addition, if you are under the age of 59½, your funds will be subject to a 10% penalty. That is not even the worst of it, either; the most expensive part of this strategy is the loss of future tax-deferred compounding on the funds you withdrew for cash flow and lost to taxes and penalties. As an example, $100,000 withdrawn could have potentially been worth over $250,000 in 20 years if it earned 5% annually. Whatever you decide to do once you're finished with this book, I advise you to strongly reconsider taking money out of your retirement plans. There are better places to get money, and together we will find them.

3. INFLATION: The one thing we can all count on sticking around.

Few people think about inflation as something that could influence the future value of their Financial *Life* Plan, but let me put it this way: I have seen clients drive to my office in cars that cost them more than their first house. College tuition is a good example. According to the Penn University Archives and Records Center, the average annual cost for college in 1955 was $500.[3] As someone who just finished his sixteenth consecutive year of paying out-of-state tuition at Purdue University for his four children, I can tell you that their laptops alone cost more than that today.

If college tuition isn't in your list of expenses, consider the postage stamp. In 1970, a stamp cost $0.06. It was up to $0.22 in 1985 and all the way to $0.46 in 2016. It's projected to cost $0.94 cents for a stamp fifteen years from now.[4] For a car, the prices have gone from an average of $3,430 in 1970 to $11,925 in 1985 to $30,812 at the time of this writing. I cringe to think that, in fifteen years, the average price of a car is projected to be $66,270.[5] Another way of looking at it is that, if inflation

---

3   Mark Frazier Lloyd and Nicholas G. Heavens, "Tuition and mandated fees, Room and Board and other educational costs at UPenn since 1900: 1950-1959," *UPenn Archives & Records Center*, 2003, http://www.archives.upenn.edu/histy/features/tuition/1950.html.

4   ING North American Insurance Corporation. 2013.

5   ING North American Insurance Corporation. 2013.

remains at a rate of 3%, then $1.00 today will buy only $0.55 worth of current goods in twenty years.

With that said, how much will everyday purchases like groceries cost twenty years from now? It would be a mistake not to take inflation into account when planning for the long-term. Inflation is the one thing we can count on sticking around.

2. PROCRASTINATION: Something we are all good at.

Let's see if any of this sounds familiar . . .

If you're between the ages of twenty-five and thirty-five, you may say, "We can't plan or save now. We're just getting started, and we don't make a lot of money yet. It takes everything we have to pay the bills and go out every now and then. Besides, our jobs are solid, and we don't plan to retire for another thirty or forty years. We have lots of time!"

If you're between the ages of thirty-five and forty-five, you might say, "Our mortgage and car payments are through the roof! Our family is growing. We need to invest in ourselves, so we can get a job promotion. When we start making more, we'll do better planning."

If you're between the ages of forty-five and fifty-five, you may say, "Kids are expensive! We spend most of our extra money on them. We work hard and deserve a good lifestyle, so we're going to enjoy that lifestyle now. We should be able to plan and save after the kids are grown."

If you're between the ages of fifty-five and sixty-five, you might say, "Retirement is right around the corner! We need to get started planning, but we've lost a job or two along the way, and our salaries are not where we thought they would be. We're just surviving. Our parents are facing health care issues that we might have to help them out with, and our kids still need some help. We can't plan or save for our future right now."

If you're over the age of sixty-five, you may say, "Where did the time go? Planning and investing sounds like a good idea, but we're sixty-five now. Our company terminated their pension plan many years ago, and Social Security is not what we thought it was going to be. We should have planned better when we were young, but it's too late now!"

Putting things off is one thing nearly everyone is good at. This is the exact opposite of what we should do when it comes to money. If you hope to avoid mistakes now while you're in transition *and* see growth in the long term, you need three things: money, return on your investments, and time. We're going to figure out how to find the money and the most prudent way to invest soon, but for now, remember that procrastination always robs you of that third essential component: time. It would be a mistake to procrastinate the preparation of your Financial *Life* Plan. Do it now.

1. NO FINANCIAL LIFE PLAN: If you don't have a destination, any road will get you there.

Could you imagine starting out on a road trip without any idea how to get to where you wanted to go? Even if you ultimately ended up where you wanted to be, there would have been a lot of unnecessary anxiety along the way, and you would have spent a lot more on gas wandering around than if you had mapped out the most efficient route before you pulled out of your driveway.

The same principle holds true about making financial decisions during a job transition without doing a Financial *Life* Plan first. This plan is like your GPS. Once it is set you know where to go to for money, how to reduce cash flow, and what rate of return you need on your investments. When you know that, then you have a better understanding of how to build a well-diversified portfolio and obtain the rate of return you needed without any more risks than necessary. With that well-diversified portfolio, you have a clear picture about what to do with your 401(k).

The Financial *Life* Plan is valuable during your job transition because it provides answers to otherwise difficult questions like the following: If you had a company car before being forced into job transition and now need to replace it, should you buy or lease? If you need to replace company life insurance that you no longer have, should you use term or whole life? Should you stop contributing to your children's college funds until you're working again and then fund a tax favorable 529 plan? Should you keep funding more of your spouse's 401(k) than necessary to get their company match as that's free money? How should you allocate your retirement funds to give you the highest probability of success without any more risks than necessary? The only way to know, and the only way to make sound, non-emotional decisions right now, is to base them on the information in your plan. The Financial *Life* Plan is your foundation for financial decisions now and forevermore.

These 10 financial mistakes are troubling enough for people who don't properly prepare their Financial *Life* Plans, but since you're in a position right now where your check engine light is blinking, any one of these mistakes can result in complete engine failure later if not properly taken care of.

Let's discuss some specific strategies for your Financial *Life* Plan that will help you avoid these 10 mistakes and engine failure. Remember, the strategies we are about to discuss can influence the way you manage your resources both now *and* when you're back working again. Steering clear of these 10 financial potholes will help take some financial stress off your shoulders, so you can focus on your job search and arrive at your financially independent destination.

CHAPTER 2

KEEPING A FULL TANK:
WHERE TO GO FOR CASH WHEN
YOU NEED IT MOST

IN THE EVENT THAT you don't have a Financial *Life* Plan just yet, let's take some time here to determine where you need to go for cash during your job transition. As you will see, not all sources for cash are created equally. There are right turns and wrong turns. Let's figure out which turns are right for you.

CHECK YOUR GPS

 Imagine that you're driving through an area of the country where your GPS is having trouble picking up a signal and your cell phone is out of service. Unfortunately, you threw out that dusty old atlas you used to keep in the trunk the day you bought your GPS-enabled

phone. Now you're in the middle of this journey, and you're not sure where to turn next.

This is a little like coming to a fork in the road without any indication of where you should go. You have two choices: You can go left or go right. Maybe the decision to go left will keep you from careening off a cliff with your short-term finances. Maybe this is the correct choice, but then again, maybe it isn't. How are you supposed to know?

What complicates the matter is that these aren't really the only two choices, are they? There is a third option. You could stop driving, pull over, and wait for the right choice to present itself. In these kinds of situations, many people just stop. They figure that their inactivity will at least ensure that they don't make any wrong turns. The trouble with this strategy is that inactivity is *itself* a wrong turn. By doing nothing, you wind up with creditors on your tail, a disastrous financial decision in your rearview mirror, and no prospects for a new job opportunity through your windshield.

When faced with a similar fork in the road toward your financial independence, it's not advantageous to come to a stop. Whether you pull over and seek advice from us or your financial coach is ultimately up to you, but the bottom line is that now is the time to take action. The sooner you speak with a financial coach, the sooner you can get back on the right road. At the very least, you can rest assured that your advisor will help you avoid a costly U-turn on the road to your financially independent destination.

TAKING A DETOUR: WHAT *NOT* TO DO WITH YOUR MONEY

When you lost your job, you probably felt desperate to ensure that your family wouldn't have to make any sacrifices while you searched for new opportunities. The first thing you possibly did was to think about how you could use your retirement plan as a supplementary source of income. In other words, in hopes of keeping your car running smoothly, you started siphoning gas from your financial tanks.

Like many people, your first move was probably to draw from the 401(k) plan you had with your former company before looking for cash elsewhere. Once your employment was terminated, the money in this account was available for the first time. Besides, you probably figured that the loss of your job meant you would have to put your retirement on hold anyway, so what good was the retirement money doing in some 401(k) plan? The IRS allows a terminated employee, due to their "separation of service," to gain access to their 401(k), and this has made that plan the easiest place to go for fast cash. *This is money I put into the plan anyway, so it's my money,* you think. *What could be the harm if I use it now, when I need it most?* You also may have figured you'd be working again soon and would be able to start putting money into a new 401(k) plan, so a few withdrawals now wouldn't be a big deal.

The next place you probably turned to is credit cards. Why wouldn't you? The constant great offers to take out new credit cards that feature either discounts in your favorite department stores or lots of free airline miles with every dollar charged are hard to pass up. You figured you could "get the plastic" by putting the new cards in your spouse's name, because she was still working and had income to put down on the application. Besides, you only had to make minimal payments each month, and you could pay them off when you were working again. Never mind that the credit card interest was five times that of a home equity line of credit, was not tax deductible, and was accumulating high-interest, nondeductible debt.

Continuing on this catastrophic financial path of family finances, you may have cashed in some stocks that had seen a nice gain from when you bought them eleven months ago. Even though the collapse of 2008 had shown you how ineffective the buy, hold, and hope strategy can be, you remained a strong proponent of the idea that the best stocks to hang on to are the ones you have held over the long term. So when you looked at your portfolio in search of cash, you avoided selling the stocks with longer-term sentimental value and instead cashed in the stocks you had held for less than a year. Unfortunately, this is a completely backwards way to go about it—cashing in stocks held for less than a year means you will have to pay taxes based on the highest marginal tax rate instead of the lower taxes at long-term capital gains rates.

Unfortunately, fear-driven decisions expose you to considerable penalties, high taxes, and some avoidable taxes on stock sales. Just as significantly, you have also compromised your long-term goal of financial independence to meet your family's short-term needs. This is like fixing the leak in your car's radiator with duct tape. It might work in the short-term, but you are going to have serious problems down the road. But not to worry. I can help you get back on track.

CHOOSING THE RIGHT PATH AT THE FORK IN THE ROAD

Job loss is a tough detour to deal with. Fortunately, there are strategies that can help keep you on the road to financial independence even while you search for a new job opportunity. While the choices you may have made did lead to some quick cash, they were all wrong turns. If you had known about how the taxes, loss of future tax-deferred compounding, and penalties incurred, you might have thought twice about the turns you took.

What you should have done is to set your GPS toward the following destinations for help with cash flow. As you consider your job transition, consider the following safer turns toward financial independence.

Severance Pay

Severance pay is often the most helpful asset when it comes to financially enduring a job transition. If you are entitled to severance, the package you can expect to receive is typically commensurate to the amount of time you had with the company. Your severance package, when used most effectively, can make the difference between having to withdraw taxable funds from your retirement accounts and not. It is important to know everything you can about your severance package, such as how to get the best package possible from your former employer and how to get the most out of the funds and benefits as you search for a new job. Your severance agreement from your past employer will tell you exactly what you can expect to receive and when.

Most people make the mistake of assuming that their agreement documentation is a final summary of what they can expect to receive. This isn't necessarily the case. There are situations where circumstances at your former employer might have changed in such a way that the benefits you can expect to receive have improved. Sometimes the stress of being terminated will prevent people from checking their agreements to make sure they are getting everything they are entitled to receive. Let's not make that mistake here.

Many people don't think about other potential sources of funds. For instance, if you traveled often (or even just recently) for your job, you may have some travel expenses that the company hasn't yet reimbursed. You might also have some unused vacation, sick, or personal days that they should pay you for. Vacation pay is part of your salary, so if you have been terminated, you may be able to get that money. Also—and this one escapes a lot of people—if you have a medical savings or flex account, do whatever you can to use that money before you lose it. If you have been putting off any doctor, dentist, or optome-trist appointments, now might be the time to take care of them.

Before we move off the topic of severance, one word about investing it—*don't*. We often have clients ask for a mutual fund with "just a little risk" to invest their severance in. A "little" bit of risk in the stock market is like being a "little" bit pregnant—impossible. Although I agree there are different levels of risk, any potential loss of principal on your severance pay is not pru-dent. Until you are working again, those funds should remain 100% liquid and safe in case it takes you a little longer to find your next career opportunity. Once you have a paycheck flowing into your bank account again, you can consider investing. For now, save your severance.

Unemployment Insurance

On the subject of cash flow, you may be eligible for unemploy-ment payments. The federal-state unemployment insurance system helps you by temporarily replacing part of your income while you look for work. Created in 1935, it is a form of social insurance in which taxes collected from employers are paid into the system on your behalf to provide you with income during your period of transition.

Each state runs its own basic unemployment insurance pro-gram, although the US Department of Labor oversees the sys-tem. The basic program in most states provides up to twenty-six weeks of benefits during transition. States provide most of the funding and pay for the actual benefits; the federal government pays only the administrative costs. Although states are subject to a few federal requirements, they are generally able to set their own eligibility criteria and benefit levels, so you'll need to check your unemployment benefits based on your state of employment.

You need to meet the following requirements to qualify for unemployment insurance benefits:

- Have lost a job through no fault of your own

- Be "able to work, available to work, and actively seeking work"

- Have earned at least a certain amount of money during a base period prior to becoming unemployed

States vary considerably in how they apply these general criteria. For example, some states do not cover part-time workers unless they are willing to take a full-time job, while other states allow these workers to qualify even if they are seeking another part-time job. You may receive unemployment benefits from the state where you were employed, even if you reside in a different state. When you apply for benefits—typically over the phone or online—the state determines whether you are eligible and the amount of benefits you qualify for. The benefits provided will vary in two respects: the number of weeks that they last and the weekly dollar amount.

Number of Weeks

While some states simply provide the same number of weeks of benefits to all unemployed workers, most states vary the number of weeks according to the amount of your past earnings, whether you had earnings in each of the four calendar quarters that make up the base period or not, and how evenly those earnings were distributed over the base period.

Dollar Amount

The average unemployment benefit is a little more than $300 per week. However, individual benefit levels vary greatly depending on the state and the amount of your previous earnings. In addition, in several states, workers receive higher benefits if they have dependents. State laws typically aim to replace about half of a worker's previous earnings up to a maximum benefit level. The maximum state-provided benefits in 2014 ranged from $235 in Mississippi (the lowest for a state) to $679 ($1,019 with dependents) in Massachusetts.

It is important to know that collecting unemployment benefits while you are working is illegal. These payments end the first day you report to work with your new employer, not when you receive your first check. Before you think, *They'll never know*, understand that state unemployment agencies match your payments to wage records and a national directory of new hire data to determine if you were working and collecting benefits at the same time.

I've had people in your situation tell me they were embarrassed to file for unemployment. Please forgive me for being so harsh, but get over it. Your employer has paid taxes to fund this program, and if you are eligible, file. It's money in your pocket, and the program is designed to chip in during your period of transition.

Checking Accounts

One of the first places to look for cash is your checking account, because it contains money that has already been taxed. Using money that has already been taxed is almost always preferable to using money that will be subject to current or future taxes. With the former, you know that what you see is what you get, while with the latter, you may wind up having to give up more of your money in taxes and penalties than you bargained for.

Savings Accounts

The money in your savings account should come next. Like your checking account, this money has already been taxed. The only reason I list it after your checking account is that your savings account does accrue some interest. Although that interest is likely minimal, it is probably more than your checking account—and every little bit helps.

Mutual Funds

After your checking and savings accounts, the next best pool to draw from is your mutual funds. The primary reason mutual funds aren't farther down the road is because they have favorable tax implications. When the money manager of your mutual funds sells some of the holdings in your fund at a gain throughout the year, you receive a tax notice at the beginning of the next year. This requires you to pay a certain amount of tax on the portion of that gain represented by your percentage of ownership. (By the way, this happens even if you did not personally sell any portion of that fund throughout the year.)

Sometimes you might be required to pay taxes on gains in your fund, even if your particular value went down. That's

never fun, but in this particular instance, the dynamic could work out in your favor. When you liquidate a portion (or all) of a mutual fund, you only have to pay taxes on the portion of gain (if any) that has not previously been taxed. This is called your *unrealized gain*, and it is often minimal, because you have already been paying taxes on this fund each year.

Stocks With a Loss

If any stocks that you own outside of your IRA, 401(k), or other retirement plan are currently worth less than what you paid for it, the IRS might provide some relief.

When a stock or other investment is sold for less than its original purchase price, then the dollar amount of difference is considered a capital loss. For tax purposes, capital losses are only reported on items that are intended to increase in value, such as the stock I am referring to here. They do not apply to items used for personal use such as planes, trains, and automobiles.

To use the loss against your income taxes, you have to *realize* the loss, which means you have to sell the investment. You can even buy it back, but you have to wait more than thirty days to do so.

From a tax perspective, you can use up to $3,000 of the loss against your earned income, which includes your severance. Anything in excess of $3,000 will be carried forward and used in future years, at the rate of $3,000, until it's all used up. In the event you sell another investment at a gain, any amount that has not been used can be accelerated and used dollar for dollar to offset the future gains at any amount.

For example, you sell an investment that has a current $10,000 loss. You can use $3,000 of that to offset the current year's income, including your salary and severance, carrying over the remaining $7,000. If you sell another investment with a gain of $7,000, you can use the $7,000 loss that you carried forward to completely offset the $7,000 gain. In the event you don't sell another investment at a gain, you can continue to use $3,000 of the carried forward loss against your earned income in future years until the $7,000 is completely used up. You'll like this part: By doing this, your losses never expire!

You are getting a "twofer" here in that first, you are liquidating some assets to help your cash flow, and second, you are getting a tax loss to help offset your salary and/or severance pay.

Tax Reporting

The IRS uses Schedule D of your 1040 tax return to compare gain and loss information reported by brokerage firms and investment companies. Schedule D allows you to report net gains and losses on your tax return, and the final net number from that form is then transposed to your individual tax return 1040 form.

Wash Sale Rules

If you liquidate an investment at a loss, you must wait at least thirty-one days after the sale date before buying the same security back if you want to deduct the loss on your tax returns. If you buy it back before that time, the loss will be disallowed under the IRS wash sale rule.[6] There are ways to circumvent the wash sale rule. Let me give you a couple of examples. When the dot-com bubble burst in 2001, we called our clients and asked, "Would you like to make some lemonade out of your lemons?"

Our clients laughed, but they were curious. Even though well-diversified portfolios were not down nearly as much as portfolios containing all dot-com type securities, such as small-cap growth funds, they were still down. We offered to sell our client's portfolios either by going into a similar portfolio right away or by cashing their portfolios out and then buying back to their original portfolio thirty-one days later. Because we were using institutionally priced "wrap" accounts, there were no transaction costs, or any other costs, associated with providing this above and beyond service. Our clients harvested losses that were then used against earned income for that year, and continued to be used at the tune of $3,000 per year, until it was either completely used or accelerated to offset something sold at a gain.

6   Stephanie Powers, "Can IRA Transactions Trigger the Wash-Sale Rule?" *Investopedia*, 2016, http://www.investopedia.com/articles/retirement/09/ira-wash-sale-rule.asp.

When we called again after the subprime mortgage debacle brought the markets down in 2007 and 2008 and asked, "Do you want to make lemonade out of lemons," our clients still laughed. They already knew where we were headed.

By the way, if you have nonqualified retirement accounts with a broker and suffered a loss in 2007 and 2008, did you get a call to make lemonade or just end up with lemons?

STOCKS WITH A GAIN

It is typically best to sell stocks held for *more* than one year if you have a gain. This is because they qualify for long-term capital gains, which is typically a much lower tax than your ordinary income tax rate. In fact, it's often 0% or 15% instead

Ordinary Rates	Long-Term Capital Gains Rates
0% or 15%	0%
25%, 28%, 33%, 35%	15%
39.6%	20%

of a 35% tax rate. Come tax season, these kinds of savings can be considerable.

As I mentioned, the gain (if any) on stocks sold that you have held for under one year is taxed at ordinary income tax rates, which is higher than the long-term capital gains tax. It's better to liquidate stocks that you've held for more than one year after those at a loss.

WHOLE LIFE INSURANCE

If you have whole life insurance with some accumulated cash values and/or dividends, you can take that cash out as a loan. Even though the insurance company charges interest on the loan, this interest typically comes at a low rate. Further, since it just reduces your death benefit, you don't even have to make monthly payments. This is a nice strategy for borrowing money without adding another bill to your expense column. Additionally, since it *is* technically a loan, it is not subject to taxes. If you have cash value life insurance and don't want to take a cash distribution from it, at least tell your insurance company to take your premiums from the cash value until you are working again.

We find that people transitioning between jobs who have whole life insurance never think of the cash value and/or dividends in their policy as a potential source of money. However, since it's tax-free and doesn't require a payment, it can be a great resource for you.

HOME EQUITY LINE OF CREDIT

Yes, a line of credit is potentially still available if you have equity in your home, your spouse is still working, and you have a good debt to income ratio with a good credit score. I know that a home equity line of credit is still debt, but it is a lower interest than what you would be paying on credit cards. Because a home equity line would be on your primary (or even your secondary) residence, the IRS allows you to deduct the interest. Since cash is king during a job transition, this allows you to keep your savings and investments intact for cash flow and emergency purposes. Once you are working again, you will want to immediately start paying off any debt,

> Cash is king during a job transition.

including this one. Even if you don't use this line of credit, it's a good thing to have just in case. If you find that you are unable to obtain one during your period of transition, put that at the top of your to-do list once you are working again, so it's in place for future emergencies and/or opportunities.

Another important point to keep in mind about home equity lines of credit is that, while the checkbook you received from the bank might look attractive to you right now, remember that you don't pay any interest on the loan until (and if) you use the funds. If you do use the funds, interest will start to be charged on the amount borrowed, and you will need to make payments.

Let's put some numbers to this as an example. If you own a $500,000 home, lenders like to see that you have some skin in the game to the tune of at least 20% ($100,000) and will loan up to 80% of the appraised value of your home ($400,000). If you currently owe $300,000, there's potentially an extra $100,000 on the table for you. I'd do this sooner than later: They take around six weeks to get. You don't want to wait until all of your other funds are depleted before you initiate the process of obtaining a line of credit on your real estate. If a line of credit was granted in this case, the lender would provide you with a checkbook and the ability to write checks up to $100,000. Beware that you may have to pay a loan origination fee plus an annual maintenance fee. However, my bank waived the origination fee and only charged $20 per year for the maintenance of the line of credit. Truth be told: They even waived that when I asked them to. You do not pay a dime in interest unless you write a check. Speaking of interest, the current rate for a home equity loan is typically below 5% and is tax deductible! Doesn't that make more sense than withdrawing funds from your 401(k) at possibly a 25% marginal tax rate and an additional 10% if you are under age 59½? A tax-deductible 5% rate versus a 35% rate should be a no-brainer!

The information I've included on home equity credit lines in this book is to say this: Even if you are unable to obtain a line of credit now due to your current job status, apply for one once you are working again. They are typically good for ten years, and you never know when an emergency will surface. While I certainly hope you never go through another job transition, statistics are not in your favor. If it does happen again, I'd rather see you have the line of credit already in place.

DEFERRED COMPENSATION

Simply stated, a nonqualified deferred compensation program is an unfunded, unsecured promise from an employer to an employee that states the employer will pay compensation at a specific time or upon a specific event in the future. The term *nonqualified* means that the plan is not required to meet most of the conditions of the Employee Retirement Income Security Act (ERISA) or the Internal Revenue Code that are imposed on tax-favored, or qualified, plans. The "future" payment is required under the Constructive Receipt Doctrine, which means the employee cannot get the funds until the future date or event, as agreed upon between the employee and employer, in order for the funds to be untaxed until they are paid out to you.

If you are covered by one of these plans, you should know that the amounts you and the company defer and the earnings are at all times *unsecured* contractual obligations of the employer. Therefore, any amounts set aside in your name are not protected from the claims of your company's general creditors. You are an unsecured general creditor of the employer, so if the company gets into financial trouble, you are not first in line.

For a nonqualified deferred compensation program, the rules for the timing of elections to defer compensation and the ability to change deferral rates are much less flexible than a typical 401(k) plan. You must choose to defer compensation before you earn the compensation, and the election timing rules differ depending upon whether the compensation is considered base pay, performance-based pay, or some other form of compensation.

An unfunded nonqualified plan operates much the same as a qualified plan for the benefit of the individual covered. As long as the individual is neither in constructive receipt of nor derives any economic benefit from the benefits or contributions accumulated under the plan, federal income tax (and generally state or other income tax) is not assessed. Rather, the individual pays taxes on the benefit received at the time of constructive or actual receipt of the plan benefits.

So if you have a deferred comp plan, here's the deal. You didn't pay tax on the money that went into the plan for you, nor its earnings. You will pay tax when you receive it, but just like the 457 plan for Government employees, there's no 10% penalty if you're younger than 59½. If you have one of these plans, check to see when your payments begin. But, before you ask—no, you will not be able to change the withdrawal dates from what was stipulated when you signed up for it.

ROTH IRA

If you meet the requirements to withdraw from your Roth IRA without a tax penalty, this is a tax- and penalty-free source of funds. Even if you have not met the requirements, you may be able to withdraw the after-tax funds you used to invest in the Roth IRA without taxes or penalties.

What are the requirements for a penalty free withdrawal? Great question. They are as follows:

- If you are over 59½, you may withdraw as much as you want so long as your Roth IRA has been open for at least five years.

- If you are under 59½, you may withdraw the exact amount of your Roth IRA contributions with no penalties.

MILE MARKER 59½

The age 59½ is an important life mile marker. Before you reach this age, if you withdraw any funds from a qualified retirement account, you will have to pay a 10% penalty in addition to taxes at your full marginal tax rate. However, since we work with many individuals who are in job transition under the age of 59½, I want to point out some exemptions to this penalty as described in IRS Publication 590.

If you have separation of service from your employer and are age 55 or older, the 10% pre–age 59½ penalty is waived for withdrawals taken from your 401(k). If you do a rollover or direct transfer to an IRA, you lose the opportunity to make these post–age 55 withdrawals without penalty.

As far as IRAs go, the IRS will not impose the pre–age 59 ½ 10% penalty as long as your withdrawals are due to the following:

- You are totally and permanently disabled.

- You are the beneficiary of a deceased IRA owner.

- The distributions are not more than your qualified higher education expenses.

- You use the distributions to buy, build, or rebuild a first home.

- The distribution is due to an IRS levy of the qualified plan.

- You are receiving distributions under IRS exemption 72(t).

- You have unreimbursed medical expenses that are more than 10% (or 7.5% if you or your spouse was born before January 2, 1951) of your adjusted gross income. The distributions are not more than the cost of your medical insurance due to a period of unemployment.

IRS 72 (T)

There is a way to get funds out of retirement accounts and avoid the 10% penalty. This strategy may not be suitable for every situation. (That's why you should always consult with a financial professional or CPA before taking action.)

From the perspective of the IRS, the day you turn 59½ is a big day. This is the age that lawmakers determined was the acceptable time for a person to be allowed to start drawing from their retirement plans without being subject to a 10% nondeductible penalty. It might seem like an arbitrary line, but it is a very clear one. If you're one day younger than 59½, that penalty applies—and believe me when I say that, in good financial times as well as bad, that nondeductible 10% penalty will hurt.

When you turn 59½, you're home free on the penalty. But keep in mind that every dollar you withdraw is still fully taxable at your ordinary income tax rates, and what you do withdraw, you can no longer earn tax-deferred compounding interest on. So when you're approaching your own plan for gathering cash during your job transition, remember that the distance you've traveled on the road of life really does matter. Mile marker 59½ is a significant one.

Here are the basics. The IRS does not allow you to use regulation 72(t) on a 401(k), only an IRA. Therefore, you will need to do a direct transfer of your 401(k) into your IRA, something we cover in greater detail later in this book. Once in the IRA, you chose one of the three income options (i.e., annuity, amortization, or straight line) based on a reasonable interest rate and your life expectancy. This choice will determine the amount you are able to receive. You have to continue to receive these payments until the *latter* of age 59½ or for five years. After either of these times, you can do whatever you want with the payments: increase them, decrease them, or stop them. What would you accomplish by doing this? You would be able to gain access to your retirement funds before the age of 59½ and avoid the IRS 10% penalty. Nice! I've used this many times when working with people like you during a job transition. 90% of the time, they didn't even know the regulation existed!

RETIREMENT PLANS

You can also draw from your 401(k), 403(b), 457, or other qualified retirement plans. You will notice that this is the last turn on the list. It is last for several reasons:

- Every dollar you withdraw is fully taxable at your ordinary income tax rates.

- If you're under the age of 59½, you'll also have to pay a 10% nondeductible penalty.

- Whatever you take out of your qualified retirement plan is no longer available to potentially grow and compound on a tax-deferred basis.

My experience from working with people in a job transition also tells me that once someone prematurely withdraws from their retirement plan, it becomes much easier for them to repeat that behavior in the future when life throws them another detour. Don't get into that habit; it can be costly.

If you are in a particularly specialized role, don't forget about your ability to earn a living on that role in the future. Some companies are willing to provide severance packages only in exchange for your willingness to sign tight noncompete agreements that could impact your ability to get a new job or work as an independent contractor in your specialty. So before you sign any paperwork, be sure to read the fine print about what you can and can't do professionally in exchange for your severance.

If you're going to enter into any post-employment discussions with your former employer, always keep your next job in mind. You're in a position where you'll have to find new work as soon as possible, so don't burn any bridges. If you leave on good terms, your former employer might be more willing to write you an effective letter of recommendation, hire you on as a consultant until you find a more permanent position elsewhere, or even help you find a new job directly. Often, employers will see these layoffs as necessary evils and will want to right the wrong by helping many of their former employees find new work.

SHARE THE ROAD

This is a difficult period, but please know that you are not traveling alone. The road ahead may have some unexpected detours, but with some good GPS guidance, you can avoid those detours. The destination of financial independence remains the same, and the journey is still worth taking. With the strategies outlined in this chapter, hopefully you have begun to think about adjustments you can make to your short-term strategies that will help keep your income at a manageable level without costing yourself too much in the long term. Now that you know where to go for cash, we can advance your journey one step further and reduce the total expenses you face each month.

Before moving on, this would be a good time to see how much you are spending. See the GPS box for how to find the cash flow calculator on our website at www.rpiplan.com /financialresourcecenter. You will find—

- A presentation that will help you understand your cash flow

- Calculators that will help you determine your current cash flow

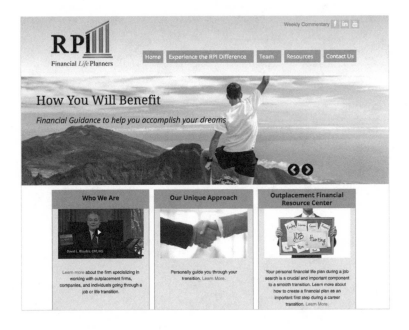

I know your period of transition has left you without the check you were accustomed to and that you have bills that need to be paid. However, where you take that money from now will have consequences later, so take it from the right place. Just because your 401(k) is available doesn't mean it should be your first choice. This would become very evident next April 15!

CHAPTER 3

GETTING A FINANCIAL TUNE-UP: HOW TO TRIM YOUR EXPENSES

SINCE THE PAYCHECK THAT you have depended on is temporarily stalled, this is a good time to look at some ways to reduce cash flow. Even though this should be an ongoing practice, we typically don't do it until we have to. It would be better for my car to change the oil more frequently than I do, but I guarantee you I'm not heading to the dealer until the "change oil" indicator light comes on. Cash flow-wise, your red light is now blinking, so let's look at some ways to potentially reduce your expenses or cash flow.

MORTGAGE REFINANCE

When we do one-on-one planning with people going through job transition, we see a lot of mortgages with interest rates substantially higher than what's currently available. Our clients typically give us reasons like, "David, I was working ten hours a day and didn't have the time to refinance."

If your rate is higher than 5%, now might be the right time to consider refinancing your mortgage. Every fraction of a percentage point you save leads to lower monthly mortgage payments. I know you are thinking, *David, I'm not working right now, no way will I be able to do anything with a loan.*

This is not always the case. You see, a lender looks not only at your ability to make your payment when it comes to real estate (loan-to-income ratio), but they also look at how much your property is worth compared to how much you owe on it, your value-to-loan ratio. They also look at your credit score and see if your spouse is working, and if so, that's a plus. If you have a decent credit score and your real estate value is more than your loan value, you may be eligible for a lower interest rate and a lower mortgage payment.

LIFE INSURANCE

I know insurance is not at the top of your mind right now, but if you have dependents and you lost your group life insurance when you lost your job, it's a necessary evil we have to discuss.

Here are a couple of basics: There are primarily two types of life insurance, whole life and term. Whole life comes in several different flavors—whole life, universal life, and variable life—and they all have a cash value component. The good news is that you have cash building up inside of your contract, and, if done right, it can be used in the future on a tax-favorable basis. However, due to this cash value buildup and, truth be told, the commissions, the premiums are substantially higher than term insurance.

Term insurance also comes in many varieties—one-, five-, ten-, or twenty-year fixed and decreasing term—but they all have the same thing in common: no cash value and less commission. So, with term insurance, the premium is substantially less than whole life.

I've often seen advisors try to obtain business by saying negative things about their competitors. That's not my style, nor does it fit my personality. Yet I feel a need to let you in on something to make sure that if you do obtain life insurance, you buy what you need instead of being sold what you don't. Term insurance costs about one-tenth of what whole life insurance costs. So if your Financial *Life* Plan says you need $100,000 of life insurance (the amount you buy should be based on what your plan says you need, not a hunch), depending on your age and health, term insurance might cost $1,000 versus whole life costing $10,000. There are times when a form of whole life makes more sense than  term, but covering your temporary insurance needs while in a job transition is not one of them! To learn more, visit our website at www.rpiplan.com. There is a calculator on our website in both the "Insurance" and "Calculator" areas titled "Assess Your Life Insurance Needs" that you can use to determine the amount of coverage you need. Once you determine the amount, there are also videos and PowerPoint presentations on the different forms of insurance that explore this topic deeper.

Since we are on the subject of life insurance, we often work with people who have some whole life insurance already in place. Often this is from a policy that was bought for them by their parents. If you have cash value built up in your policy, you don't have to wait to die to benefit from your insurance. Whole life insurance contains a loan provision that will allow you to borrow your cash value out of your contract. Now before you get all negative on me over "borrowing," get this: You don't have to pay it back during your life! For example, if you have a whole life policy with a death benefit of $100,000 and cash value of $10,000, you can borrow the $10,000 now, and at death your beneficiaries will receive $90,000 as the loan will be deducted from the death payment. I should also tell you that the insurance company will charge interest on the loan, but it's typically a nominal rate and can also be paid back at death. You always have the option of paying the loan back to the insurance company after you are working again if desired. Bottom line is that you are concerned about cash flow today, not your death benefit years from now.

You should also check to see if your whole life insurance policy pays a dividend and, if so, where is that dividend going? If the insurance agent checked a box on the application to "have future dividend payments purchase additional life insurance," then each time a dividend is paid, you are buying more insurance (and the agent is getting a new commission). I would suggest having that dividend paid out to you instead, or even have it reduce your premium so that you have to pay less out of your current cash flow.

For some additional tips for streamlining your expenses visit

 www.rpiplan.com/resource-center/insurance

our website at: www.rpiplan.com/resource-center/insurance. You will find—

- A calculator to determine if you need insurance

- Articles like "Assess Life Insurance Needs," "Is Term Life Insurance for You?" and "Term Insurance Is the Simplest Form of Life Insurance: Here's How It Works"

- PowerPoint presentations such as—

  ○ "Term vs. Permanent Life Insurance"

  ○ "What Are Your Options: Term and Permanent Insurance"

CARS: WHETHER TO LEASE OR BUY

If you need a new car—maybe you're replacing a company car to which you no longer have access—consider leasing instead of buying. When you lease, often you don't have to come up with a down payment. Remember, right now cash is king.

We often see clients turn to being a consultant during job transition, either as a temporary solution to cash flow or as a new career choice. If you entertain business clients, leasing allows you to drive a luxury vehicle for less money (and there may be a tax write-off for certain professions). Others just like to drive a brand new car every two or three years. Leasing isn't only a dollars-and-cents question; it's about personal tastes and priorities. Let's take a closer look at leasing vs. buying.

The Advantages and Disadvantages of Leasing a Car

Leasing a car has several advantages and disadvantages. Some of the advantages are—

- Lower or no down payment

- Lower monthly payments

- The ability to drive a *better* car for *less* money each month

- Lower repair costs (with a three-year lease, the factory warranty covers most repairs)

- The ability to drive a new car every two or three years

- No trade-in hassles at the end of the lease

- Lower sales tax (only on the portion of the car you finance.[7])

Leasing a car also has its disadvantages. They include—

- Not owning the car at the end of the lease

- Limited mileage (typically 12,000 to15,000 miles a year; you pay extra if you go over your allowed annual average)

- Confusing lease contracts

- Leasing is more expensive in the long run (as opposed to buying and driving until the wheels fall off)

- Wear-and-tear charges can add up (must be paid at lease termination)

- Costly early termination fees

The Advantages and Disadvantages of Buying a Car

If you are considering buying a car, you should look at the advantages and disadvantages, so you can make an informed decision, just as you did with leasing. The advantages of buying a car include the following:

- Pride of ownership—you can modify your car as you please

- Long-term cost effectiveness

---

7   Scott Drenkard, "Sales and Local Tax Rates in 2014," *Tax Foundation*, March 18, 2014, http://taxfoundation.org/article/state-and-local-sales-tax-rates-2014.

- No penalties for excess mileage

- Increased flexibility—you can easily sell the car whenever you want

There are also disadvantages to buying a car:

- Higher down payment, difficult when you are trying to preserve your cash

- Higher monthly payments

- Maintenance costs once the warranty expires

- Trade-in or selling hassles when you're ready to get rid of your car

- Ready cash is tied up in a car, which depreciates over time, rather than an investment that appreciates with time

The bottom line is that leasing makes it easier to preserve your cash and get more car for less money. You are essentially paying for a portion of the car, instead of buying the entire vehicle. We have a "lease vs. buy" calculator at www.rpiplan.com that will help you determine which technique makes the most financial sense for you.

 www.rpiplan.com/resource-center/lifestyle

For additional tips on buying versus leasing visit our website at www.rpiplan.com/resource-center/lifestyle:

- "Should I Buy or Lease an Auto?" Calculator

- "Buying vs. Leasing a Car" Article

SAVING FOR COLLEGE FUNDS

Let me tell you right from the start that this section, as well as the one that follows, can be controversial if you don't read the entire section. Why controversial? I'm going to suggest you consider suspending your savings for your children's college funds. You could read one hundred books on financial planning, and all of them would tell you to start saving for college the day your children are born, because it's so expensive and the annual inflation rate applied to college tuition is substantially higher than traditional inflation. A good tool to reference is www.usinflationcalculator.com. It states that college tuition increases annually at two and a half times the standard inflation rate. Trust me, I know how expensive college is. I just finished paying sixteen years of out-of-state tuition for my four kids to go to Purdue! However, if your children are not heading off to college anytime soon, allocating your current assets for a future expense is not their best use. Here's the preferred order of funding:

1. Suspend current funding for future college needs.

2. Complete a Financial *Life* Plan that includes how much needs to be saved monthly to meet your stipulated college funding goals.

3. Start your new job.

4. Establish a 529 College plan in your home state and start saving the amount your plan and cash flow ability dictate.

Now, I want to make sure you read this section correctly. I did not say to *permanently* stop college funding, just temporarily.

CREATING A 529 PLAN

A 529 plan is an education savings plan operated by a state or educational institution designed to help you save money for future college costs. It is named after Section 529 of the IRS Code, which created these types of savings plans in 1996. These plans can be used to meet the costs of colleges nationwide and are not restricted to just your state. They offer great income tax breaks. Your investment grows tax-deferred, and distributions to pay for the beneficiary's college costs come out tax-free as long as the funds are used for educational purposes. (Sorry, season tickets for sporting events don't qualify.) Tax-free treatment for 529 plans was made permanent with the Pension

Protection Act of 2006. Your own state may offer some tax breaks as well (like an upfront deduction for your contributions or income exemption on withdrawals) in addition to the federal treatment.

You, the donor parent, stay in control of the 529 account. With few exceptions, your child has no rights to the funds, so if they decide to use the funds to start a rock band, you can stop it. You are the one who calls the shots; you decide when withdrawals are taken and for what purpose. A 529 plan even allows you to reclaim the funds for yourself or other family members any time you desire, no questions asked. (However, the earnings portion of the "nonqualified" withdrawal will be subject to income tax and an additional 10% penalty tax if not used for educational purposes.) Compare this level of control to a custodial account under the Uniform Transfers to Minors Acts (UTMA) and you will find the 529 plan gives you much more say in how your investment is used.

A 529 plan can provide you with a very easy way to save for your children's college. You complete a simple enrollment form and make your contribution (or sign up for automatic deposits). You can also check a box so the allocation automatically lowers your percentage of equities each year as your child gets closer to needing the money for college. Then, you can relax and forget about it if you like. The ongoing investment of your account is handled by the plan, not by you.

With a 529 plan, you won't receive a Form 1099 to report taxable or nontaxable earnings until the year you make withdrawals.

Again, the earnings are tax-free as long as you use the funds for a qualified educational purpose such as tuition, room and board, and books.

If you want to move your investment around, you may change to a different option in a 529 savings program every year, program permitting, or you may roll over your account to a different state's program, provided no such rollover for your beneficiary has occurred in the prior twelve months. Hint: There is no federal limit on the frequency of these changes if you replace the account beneficiary with another qualifying family member at the same time.

Something else that is great to know: Everyone is eligible to take advantage of a 529 plan, and you can put in substantial amounts. Generally, there are no income limitations or age restrictions.

I'd like to make sure you know something else here: You do not have to use the 529 plan of your state. As an example, I live in Illinois, but if I like the 529 plan of another state better, I can use it. Remember, the 529 plan is named after its section number in the *federal*, not state, tax code. However, if you use a 529 plan in a different state than what you reside in, you may have to pay state tax on the annual earnings of the account. Additionally, some state 529 plans pay commissions to brokers, so if someone is recommending a different state's 529 plan, make sure the recommendation is in your best tax interest.

To give you an idea about this plans' flexibility, I set up 529 plans for my four kids using the Illinois 529 plan (where we live) even though they all four went to Purdue University in Indiana. When Bridgette graduated, there were funds left over in her plan, so I transferred them to her younger sister, Lauren. When Lauren graduated, we transferred the leftover funds to Megan's 529 plan, and when Megan graduated, her leftover funds got transferred to her brother JD's 529 plan. Now that JD has graduated, and we still have funds in our 529 plan, we will split the remaining funds equally among our four kids, so the money can be used for their future kids, such as Bridgette's recently born daughter Brooke Nicole. Susan, my wife, and I even have the flexibility of using our leftover 529 funds for higher education for ourselves. There's a lot of flexibility.

When each of our kids graduated high school, my wife and I gave them a laptop for their graduation gift, as college work is now completed and submitted via the Internet. My kids still have a hard time believing I used a typewriter to submit my papers! For those of you with a little gray hair, remember those white "corrective" strips we'd insert after we backspaced over a typing error? When they finally came out with a portable typewriter with that built in, I thought I had seen the end of technology advancement! Anyway, due to a recent change, 529 plan funds can now be used to purchase that college-bound laptop.

For additional information on college funding, visit our website, www. rpiplan.com. If you use the "Saving for College" calculator in the "Investment" section of calculators, be sure to have a bottle of wine

www.rpiplan.com

opened first and remember this story from the dad that wrote this book.

Several years ago, a neighbor of mine made a comment that he would not have to pay a cent toward the college cost for his three kids because their grandparents had funded 100% of it. I thought of that every time I wrote all thirty-two semester tuition checks for the sixteen years my kids went through college. As I sat in Purdue's Elliot Hall for the fourth time during JD's graduation on May 14, 2016, I had a private teary-eyed moment thinking of how great it felt to have helped provide our four kids with a college degree, something that will help them for the rest of their careers and give them the confidence to succeed. Long after my wife and I are gone, they will always know we worked and sacrificed to do that for them. At that moment, I thought of my friend who talked about not having to pay a cent toward his children's college cost and felt sorry for him. I share this memory because I hope it will help you have a positive attitude toward the hard work and sacrifice you will endure if you assist your kids with their college education. Just like their college degree is something no one can take away from them, the feeling you will have from helping them obtain that degree is something no one will ever be able to take away from you. So as soon as you are working again, let's get that 529 plan funded!

SHOULD YOU SUSPEND SAVING FOR YOUR SPOUSE'S RETIREMENT?

When I mentioned the suspension of college funding, I indicated that your spouse suspending their 401(k) contributions would be controversial. Advisors are typically so programmed to tell you to invest in retirement plans as early in life as possible that it almost feels immoral to advise you not to. However, specializing in working with those in transition either between jobs or into retirement, I have conditioned myself to look at the total picture instead of just the retirement picture. Like most, I'm sure you have more time-sensitive issues than your future retirement, like making a mortgage payment next month. Therefore, we often recommend your spouse *temporarily* (notice I keep using that term) stop their payroll deductions into their 401(k) plan or at least reduce the contributions down to the limit that the employer matches. I know that reference to employer matching caught a couple of you off guard, so let me explain. If your employer provides a match, let's say 50% up to a maximum of 6% of your contribution, that means they will give you 3% as long as you are putting at least 6% of your salary into your 401(k). That's free money, so I'm not suggesting your spouse completely stop their 401(k) contributions. Rather, I'm encouraging them to contribute just above the amount you need to get the entire free match that's available from your employer.

With a proper road map, which will be provided by your Financial *Life* Plan, you'll know not only what sources to use first for cash flow and how to reduce your expenses, but you will also know exactly how much you need to save for your longer-term goals, such as retirement, and how to invest those funds, which you and your spouse can start doing once you're working again. Here's something that you might find reassuring. The probability of financial success *increases* when the amount invested in the 401(k) and the diversified allocation is based on your long-term Financial *Life* Plan even though the amount invested *decreased* short-term during your period of transition. Therefore, a temporary suspension of your or your spouse's 401(k) plan does not automatically result in you not being able to reach your goals.

UNDERSTANDING POSSIBLE TAX DEDUCTIONS

Did you know the IRS allows you to potentially deduct many expense items from your job search? Of course, I'm not a CPA and cannot give tax advice, but I urge you to look at the following list of some of the items that could potentially be tax deducted and consult with your tax advisor for a final determination. You should be aware of these potential items so that you can keep receipts and for tax time. Additionally, if something like a new iPad is in your future, you may want to purchase it while you are in transition for potential tax-deductible reasons. The following is a brief list of possible deductible fees:

- Equipment that allows you access to the Internet for job searches such as computers, iPads, phones, and Internet service

- Outplacement agency fees

- Employment agency fees

- Costs of creating and printing your resume

- Cost of advertising your services

- Office supplies

- Physical exam required for employment

- Newspapers for classifieds

- Expenses related to resume preparation

- Career counseling expenses

- Legal fees to review employment contracts

- Licenses and regulatory fees

- Telephone expenses to prospective employers

- Training materials, training classes, and travel

Job Search Expenses Can Be Tax Deductible

IRS Summertime Tax Tip 2012-06, July 18, 2012

SUMMERTIME IS THE SEASON that often leads to major life decisions, such as buying a home, moving, or making a job change. If you are looking for a new job that is in the same line of work, you may be able to deduct some of your job-hunting expenses on your federal income tax return.

Here are seven things the IRS wants you to know about deducting costs related to your job search:

1. To qualify for a deduction, your expenses must be spent on a job search in your current field. You may not deduct expenses you incur while looking for a job in a new field.

2. You can deduct employment and outplacement agency fees you pay while looking for a job in your present field. If your employer pays you back in a later year for employment agency fees, you must include the amount you received in your gross income, up to the amount of your tax benefit in the earlier year.

3. You can deduct amounts you spend for preparing and mailing copies of your resume to prospective employers as long as you are looking for a new job in your present field.

4. If you travel to look for a new job in your current field,

you may be able to deduct travel expenses to and from the area to which you traveled. You can only deduct the travel expenses if the trip is primarily to look for a new job. The amount of time you spend on personal activity unrelated to your job search compared to the amount of time you spend looking for work is important in determining whether the trip is primarily personal or is primarily to look for a new job.

5. You cannot deduct your job search expenses if there was a substantial break between the end of your last job and the time you begin looking for a new one.

6. You cannot deduct job search expenses if you are looking for a job for the first time.

7. In order to be deductible, the amount that you spend for job search expenses, combined with other miscellaneous expenses, must exceed a certain threshold. To determine your deduction, use Schedule A, Itemized Deductions. Job search expenses are claimed as a miscellaneous itemized deduction. The amount of your miscellaneous deduction that exceeds 2% of your adjusted gross income is deductible.

For more information about job search expenses, see IRS Publication 529, Miscellaneous Deductions. This publication is available on IRS.gov or by calling 800-TAX-FORM (800-829-3676).

CHOOSING HEALTH INSURANCE

You are probably aware of the Consolidated Omnibus Budget Reconciliation Act, or COBRA. This is a federal law that entitles you to buy into the same health coverage your employer used to provide you, as long as you were enrolled in their plan while working, for up to eighteen months. This is not automatic, you have to elect in within sixteen days of being notified you are eligible by your employer. In some cases, your employer will continue to pay their share of the premium. However, more often than not, the full cost, plus an administrative fee of up to 2% of the premium, falls onto your checkbook. I have seen people in job transition opt out of their employer plan through COBRA and it turned out to be a mistake. Many that opt out think they can replace their old employer plan on a more cost-efficient basis, or they opt out for emotional reasons, as they have negative feelings about their past employer and want nothing to do with them, including their health insurance.

In most cases, your employer's group insurance covers many lives, so the premiums are more reasonable than an individual policy due to the discounts inherent with large groups. Furthermore, when many lives are insured, individual health issues become less of an issue to the insurer, and ultimately the premium, as the poor health of one person is offset by the good health of many.

If you are married and your spouse is working, you might be able to get covered under your spouse's health insurance, so be sure to compare the cost of doing that to your COBRA.

You should also check health insurance options under the 2010 Patient Protection and Affordable Care Act, affectionately known as Obamacare. Here is the link, in case you wish to look into this further: www.healthcare.gov.

So how do expensive health insurance premiums fall into a chapter on trimming expenses? I've placed it here, because adding yourself to your spouse's insurance, Obamacare, or COBRA can potentially be less expensive than an individual policy. Do your research before you opt out.

I know I have asked you to consider some things in this chapter that may go against everything you have ever read, such as suspending investments for your children's education and your retirement. Remember, though, that I have used the term *temporary* if your personal Financial *Life* Plan supports it. Often we will actually end up with a plan that increases the probability of success for accomplishing your long-term goals even though you temporarily stopped funding some of them. You can become more successful than what you were on track for prior to the job loss and suspension of funding. Why? Because your personal Financial *Life* Plan supported taking advantage of tax favorable 529 plans and retirement plan investment allocations that were designed to obtain the rate of return your Financial *Life* Plan said you needed and without any more risks than necessary. Add some periodic maintenance in the form of an annual review and "tweaking" the plan and portfolio to the goal, and many times the result can be arriving at your destination even sooner than originally planned!

> **In essence, your Financial *Life* Plan becomes your GPS!**

In essence, your Financial *Life* Plan becomes your GPS!

Trimming our expenses is something we should do all of the time, but we don't. We typically need to face a crisis before we take a hard look at our budget. In addition to the suggestions just given in this chapter, visit our website, www.rpiplan.com. Once there, go

to the cash flow calculator found in the Financial Resource Center and type in your expenses. A second after you hit the submit button, you will have a complete report of where every dollar is going in a numeric report supplemented with a color graph, resulting in the identification of expenses that can be reduced or eliminated. At this time of transition, that's powerful stuff!

I've worked with people in transition for over twenty-five years. From a practical "what works" perspective, I have noted those in transition do better with expense reductions vs. eliminations. I'll use coffee as an example.

If you are in the habit of driving to your favorite coffee shop every morning and buying an expensive cup of coffee, you will have greater difficulty eliminating that vs. driving to a different coffee shop that charges much less for a cup of coffee. Maintaining your routines is important. Additionally, the more radical changes you have to make in your lifestyle, the more discontent you'll be during your job transition. If cash flow allows, look for ways to reduce expenses instead of completely eliminating them. Vacations can continue, just take a road trip instead of a flight to an expensive resort. Friday night dinners out can continue, but try out new pizza places in place of expensive restaurants. Although I use coffee and pizza as examples, you can, and should, apply this idea to every expense. Remember to maintain a positive attitude throughout this process, as it will reflect in everything you do, including how your body handles the increased stress you are under, how your relationships stay with the closest people around you, and how you perform in future interviews.

CHAPTER 4

EXTEND THE WARRANTY ON YOUR 401(K): HOW TO PROTECT YOUR LARGEST INVESTMENT

HAVE YOU EVER HEARD your GPS say, "Turn hard left" instead of just saying, "Turn left?" When you look at the GPS or the road ahead, you see that you can not only turn left or right, but you actually have two left or two right turn options, one sharp and one at more of a slight angle? Well now that you have separated from your employer, the IRS says you have four options with your 401(k) plan. Four turning options, and if you take the wrong turn, you will be heading away from your financially independent destination. Your company retirement plans potentially represent one of your largest assets; this is one of the most important chapters in this book.

Before starting, I'm going to refer to a company retirement plan as a 401(k), but most of the same rules apply with a pension lump sum, 403(b) if you are a teacher or employee of a nonprofit organization, or a 457 plan if you are a government employee as well as similar retirement plans.

My intent is to educate you about the advantages and disadvantages of each option without making a blanket recommendation. Every situation is different, and you'll need to consider your personal situation before making a choice. Imagine if you went to a doctor's office and he said, "I'm sorry, I'm running late and don't have time to evaluate you. Here's a prescription, just take this medicine."

Hopefully you would not take the pills and be very leery of his advice. Likewise, if someone immediately tells you that you should do a rollover of your 401(k) into an investment of their choice, without discussing the pros and cons of all four of your

 options and their fees and without an analysis of your financial situation and needs, you would be just as leery of their advice as the doctor's. You need to understand the advantages and disadvantages of each option and choose the one that fits your situation. Don't take this major decision lightly.

OPTION 1: LEAVE THE FUNDS WITH YOUR PREVIOUS EMPLOYER

Advantages

There are some advantages to this option:

It's Easy

The money is already in place. You still need to make sure the money is properly allocated based on what your Financial *Life* Plan says will give you the highest probability of success without any more risks than necessary. This option simply means you do not need to move the funds.

It Has Low Fees

There may be fewer internal fees with your old employer than investments outside the plan. I have had individuals tell me they did not have any fees associated with their 401(k) plan. On the contrary, all investments have fees associated with them, you just may not be aware of them. If you are invested in any mutual fund, that fund will have internal management fees. Even index and exchange-traded funds (ETF) are managed by someone who is rightfully paid for their work. However, the fees with your old employer may be less than similar investments outside the plan and typically do not involve an additional advisory fee.

The Age 55 Rule

The IRS allows you to withdraw funds from a retirement plan, such as a 401(k), after you have been "separated from service" and have attained the age of 55, without incurring the normal 10% pre–age 59½ penalty. Don't misunderstand here. The withdrawals are still fully taxed, meaning you'll still need to pay Uncle Sam his share and any money that goes to the IRS is no longer in your account, eliminating any potential future growth on those funds. It's just the 10% pre–age 59½ penalty that is forgiven.

Retaining Extra Services

Your 401(k) plan might provide access to investment advice, planning tools, telephone help lines, educational materials, and workshops. If your former employer offers these extra services, they usually come without any additional costs.

Keeping Company Stock

If your employer allows you to purchase company stock in your 401(k) plan, you are probably making those stock purchases free of any commissions. With that said, don't forget the advantages of diversification outweigh the commissions saved on this stock purchase. I've read that last sentence back to myself several times, and my wording does not reflect the negative impact I have witnessed for people who have failed to diversify their portfolio. The age-old story of the boiling frog comes to mind. The poor frog sits in a pan of water on a stove top with the burner on low. As the water slowly gets warmer and warmer, the frog fails to jump out, and then it's too late. Like the frog, many people have a false sense of security when it comes to the stock of the company they have worked at for many years. Additionally, just like the frog that fails to jump out of the water, the excess accumulation of stock happens over many years by investing in it as part of their 401(k) and by the person purchasing more because the stocks are commission free. Before you know it, the water is boiling and it's too late for you to diversify as a sudden and long-lasting reduction in the stock price has eroded 50% or more of your retirement assets.

Protecting Yourself from Creditors

If you are in a high liability career, such as the medical field, you should know that generally speaking 401(k) plan assets have superior protection from creditors under federal law.

Keeping Your Assets Liquid

Once you have entered your job transition, you can withdraw your 401(k) anytime you want. People often think if they don't transfer the funds out of their 401(k) within a certain time period, they lose the ability to do so later. This is normally not the case.

Disadvantages

Keeping your funds with your previous employer has some disadvantages:

Having Limited Investment Options

Most 401(k) plans have ten to twenty investment options. They are sometimes designed for convenience, and you must allocate among only the fund choices offered in your plan. However, my experience has been that, even with limited investment options in which to choose from, there are enough to do a basic asset allocation.

Lacking Investment Recommendations

You will be responsible for choosing and managing investment options with your 401(k) plan. Do you have the training for this? Do you know how to properly diversify your portfolio? I recall reviewing a portfolio in 2003 that the investor stated was well diversified among several funds, so I couldn't understand how he had lost so much money in 2002. When I analyzed his funds, I discovered all the funds they had chosen were small-cap growth funds. When this particular asset class fell out of favor, as it did in 2001 and 2002, he didn't have any other asset classes in the portfolio to help counter the correction that small-cap growth technology companies took.

Not Taking Old 401(k) Plans into Account with Current Planning

I've seen individuals do a Financial *Life* Plan, determine how their investments should be diversified, and be very diligent about investing their current assets accordingly, but then they forget to do the same with their previous 401(k) plan. Don't "set it and forget it." In yet another example, when it comes to taking your required minimum distributions (RMD) at age 70½, you have to withdraw a percentage of your previous year's December 31 balance, which is currently 3.65%. If you do not take your full RMD, the tax penalty on the amount not withdrawn is taxed at—are you ready for this—50%. If you keep your 401(k) plan with your previous employer, don't forget about it!

Being in a Blackout Period

If your company decides to change their 401(k) administrator, you will enter into something they refer to as a *blackout period*. Your 401(k) administrator will often freeze your account until the assets can be reconciled and moved to the new 401(k) administrator. In some cases, this can take several weeks. During this period, you can't make any changes to your investments. However, the blackout period is well communicated in advance, so you can make sure your allocations are the way you want them to be prior to entering the blackout period, but the inability to make any changes during that time is still a disadvantage.

No 72(t) Exclusion

In an IRS 72(t) exclusion, you do not have to pay the 10% penalty on retirement funds withdrawn prior to age 59½. You cannot take advantage of the 72(t) to avoid the 10% penalty if the funds are kept in the 401(k).

No Option to Convert to a Roth IRA

I often see individuals in a low tax bracket the year they are transitioned out of their job due to their reduced income. If their situation is such, it might make sense to do a Roth IRA conversion for a host of possible reasons, such as knowing they'll be receiving large deferred compensation payouts in the future, making their tax bracket higher. When the funds are directly transferred to your IRA, you declare it to be a Roth on the application. Although this results in having to pay taxes on the conversion during the year in which you convert, you can withdraw the funds after five years and age 59½ on a tax-free basis. You do not have this option if the funds are left in your 401(k).

Making Emotional Decisions

People can be hesitant to leave their funds with their previous employer for emotional reasons. I recall one person saying to me, "Why should I keep my money with the company that didn't keep me?" Although I understand this sentiment, I would encourage you to take the emotions out of the equation and make the decision that fits your situation the best, even if it means leaving your 401(k) with a company you are upset with.

OPTION 2: ROLL YOUR 401(K) INTO YOUR NEXT EMPLOYER'S 401(K)

If your next employer allows it, you may be able to roll over your current 401(k) into the 401(k) of your next employer. Over the years, I've been asked about something countless times that I want to address up front: If you transfer your 401(k) from your recent employer into the 401(k) of your next employer, your new employer will not match any of those funds with a matching contribution. You are probably smiling right now thinking how obvious that is, but yes, I've had people think they would get a match. Here's how that played out. The individual we were working with got a new job with a company that offered a 3% match dollar for dollar on the first 3% of employee contributions. They had a 401(k) from a previous employer valued at approximately $500,000. They thought the new employer would give them 3% of the $500,000, or $15,000, if they transferred their old 401(k) into the new company's 401(k). No, you do not receive a penny of match on assets transferred to your new 401(k), only on new contributions that come out of your new paychecks. Also, it's important to keep your funds in a separate IRA if you plan on directly transferring them to your next employer. If you "comingle" your 401(k) with other IRA funds, you lose the ability to transfer the 401(k) funds to your next employer.

This option has some advantages.

Advantages

Consolidated Accounts

Transferring your old 401(k) into your new company's 401(k) would result in the consolidation of both accounts, making them easier to monitor.

Required Minimum Distributions (RMD)

Once you reach 70½, the rules for both 401(k) plans and IRAs require annual taxable withdrawals of around 3.65% annually. If you are still working at age 70½, you are generally not required to make these distributions from your current employer's 401(k) plan. Therefore, the assets from your previous 401(k) that were transferred to your next employer's 401(k) may escape the RMD requirements if you are still working at that same company at age 70½.

Loan Provisions

Your next employer's 401(k) plan will probably have loan provisions. Although there are advantages and disadvantages with borrowing from a 401(k), it may at least be an option.

Lower Advisory Fees

Just as with your past employer's 401(k) plan, your next employer's plan may have investment options with lower fees. Unless you have an advisor charging you to assist with your allocations, you can avoid paying an advisory fee.

Disadvantages

All of the disadvantages listed with keeping your 401(k) at your past employer would be the same if you transferred your funds to your next employer's 401(k). Not all employer 401(k) plans allow old 401(k) funds to be rolled into them. Therefore, you may keep the funds in the existing 401(k) plan while waiting for the next job and 401(k) plan, only to learn you cannot roll your old funds into your new one.

OPTION 3: TAXABLE DISTRIBUTION

This option reminds me of Tom Cruise in the movie *Jerry Maguire* when he says, "Show me the money."

Following are the advantages of this option.

Advantages

Access to Funds

After you leave your former company and withdraw your 401(k), you have access to your funds for up to 60 days before you have to roll them over into an IRA to avoid taxation. Generally, the 60-day rollover deadline cannot be extended. However, the IRS has the limited authority to waive the deadline under certain extraordinary circumstances, such as when external events prevent you from completing the rollover by the rollover deadline. To apply for a waiver, you must file a private letter ruling request with the IRS. A nonrefundable user fee must accompany these requests. For more information, see IRS Publication 590-A. Also, if you are helping a parent that was born before January 1, 1936, and they receive a lump sum distribution that they do not rollover, special rules for calculating the amount of the tax on the payment might apply to them. See IRS Publication 575 for additional information.

Having access to the funds for 60 days is the only advantage I can think of, but I have no problem thinking of many disadvantages of this option, as I have seen so many people get into trouble using it. So here goes.

Disadvantages:

20% Will Be Withheld

Even if you roll your funds over to a new employer's plan or IRA within the mandated 60 days, 20% of your qualified plan will be withheld.

Taxed as Income

Whatever amount you do not roll over into an IRA within 60 days will be taxed at your full ordinary tax rate. Well, if the IRS is holding 20% of your 401(k) as a withholding tax, that's a problem isn't it? You have to roll over 100% if you don't want to pay any tax, but you are left with only 80%. This means you have to beg, borrow, or steal (please know that's humor) that 20% to ensure that the amount you are rolling over matches the total of your old 401(k) account so that you roll over 100% of your 401(k). If your 401(k) was $100,000, you only received $80,000, and the IRS was sent the other $20,000 as a withholding tax, then you need to make sure that you have an additional $20,000 to make up the difference. When I see people take a direct distribution, it's normally due to their lack of understanding the consequences or because they checked a wrong box on a form. However, once they have to pull 20%, or in this example, $20,000 from their savings to add to the 80%, or $80,000, they know to never make the same mistake again. Remember, cash is king, so the last thing you should be doing right now is taking money from your savings to make up for the amount of your

401(k) that was sent to the IRS as a withholding tax. To be fair here, I do want to point out that you will get that 20% back from the IRS when you file your tax return for the year in which the withholding tax was paid on your behalf. For example, if you took a direct distribution from your 401(k) in April of 2016, and the IRS took a 20% withholding tax and you made that up out of your savings to do a complete rollover, you would get the 20% back when you filed your tax return by April 15, 2017. What interest rate will the IRS pay you on your money that they held for that year? You guessed it—none, zero, nada!

10% Pre-age 59½ Penalty

Not only will any funds not rolled over within 60 days be fully taxed, you'll also have to pay an additional 10% penalty if you're younger than 59½.

One Rollover per Year Rule

The IRS says that you can only do one IRA rollover per year. Let's say you take a direct distribution of your 401(k), make up the 20% that was withheld for taxes and sent to the IRS in your behalf, and roll over 100% of your previous 401(k) balance. Then, you find a mutual fund a friend recommends, and within 60 days, you roll all of your 401(k) funds into it. Afterward, you update your resume and start your job search. A few months later, you get a job offer and are told that you start bright and early on a Monday a couple of weeks out. With a new job secured, you now turn your attention back to the fund that you rolled your 401(k) plan into a few months earlier. You research and find the right home for those funds distributed, just like you previously did when you took the funds out of your 401(k). You decided to roll over the funds from the old stock your friend told you about to the new "hot" investment you found. Knowing about the 60 day over rule from when you rolled these funds the first time, you take no chances and actually roll them into the new investment the same day you withdraw the funds from the old IRA. All good? Not even close. You violated the one rollover per year rule, and the entire amount will be subject to tax. Most people that take this disastrous turn find it gets even bumpier as they continue down this road. They don't know they violated this rule until the IRS catches up to them, which is normally around two years after the fact (before the three-year statute of limitations expires). What does this mean? It means two years of interest on top of the tax due on the full amount of the IRA rollover and a 10% penalty if you are under age 59½. This could easily result in the loss of half of your IRA and, potentially, many years of tax-deferred compounding on those funds you lost to the IRS in taxes and penalties. This would be a major accident on your road to financial independence.

Consolidation

Don't speed-read this one, because it's really important. As if this one rollover per year rule couldn't get worse, it did due to a recent court ruling. This is where the "all IRAs are now consolidated for this one rollover per year rule" comes in. Starting January 1, 2015, the IRS adopted a new rule and only allows taxpayers to do one rollover per year, no matter how many IRAs the person has. This rule was first adopted in the tax court case Bobrow v. Comm'r, T.C. Memo. 2014-21. Thus, starting in 2015, a person with two or more IRAs is restricted to doing one rollover for all the IRAs he or she owns during any 365-day period (IRS Announcement 2014–15). Note that the 365-day period is not determined on a calendar-year basis. Instead, it starts when you receive the distribution.

I'll use an example to help clarify this, as it's a big deal. Let's stick with my last example where a person took a direct distribution from their 401(k) plan, made up the 20% that was withheld for taxes, and within 60 days rolled the funds into an IRA in their name. Now to incorporate this new "consolidation" rule, let's say they also had a $2,000 IRA invested in another mutual fund. In order to keep things easy, they decided to take that $2,000 IRA as a distribution and, just like they did with their 401(k), roll the funds into the same place they put their 401(k) within 60 days. At this point, they have only rolled their 401(k) once and the $2,000 IRA once. However, since the IRS now consolidates all IRAs as one, they will consider the second rollover of the $2,000 to be part of the 401(k) rollover, meaning you have now done two rollovers in one year. If your original 401(k) rollover was $100,000 and the second rollover was $2,000, you now have to pay tax and penalties on $102,000! If your 401(k) was $500,000 and the second IRA rollover was $2,000, how much is now taxed and potentially penalized? That's right, $502,000!

Application of One-Per-Year Limit
on IRA Rollovers Announcement 2014–15

THIS ANNOUNCEMENT ADDRESSES THE application to Individual Retirement Accounts and Individual Retirement Annuities (collectively, "IRAs") of the one-rollover-per-year limitation of § 408(d)(3)(B) of the Internal Revenue Code and provides transition relief for owners of IRAs. Section 408(d)(3)(A)(i) provides generally that any amount distributed from an IRA will not be included in the gross income of the distributee to the extent the amount is paid into an IRA for the benefit of the distributee no later than 60 days after the distributee receives the distribution. Section 408(d)(3)(B) provides that an individual is permitted to make only one rollover described in the preceding sentence in any one-year period. Proposed Regulation § 1.408-4(b)(4)(ii) and IRS Publication 590, Individual Retirement Arrangements (IRAs), provide that this limitation is applied on an IRA-by-IRA basis. However, recent tax court opinion based on Bobrow v. Commissioner, T.C. Memo 2014-21, held that the limitation applies on an aggregate basis, meaning that an individual could not make an IRA-to-IRA rollover if he or she had made such a rollover involving any of the individual's IRAs in the preceding one-year period. The IRS anticipates that it will follow the interpretation of § 408(d)(3)(B) in Bobrow and, accordingly, intends to withdraw the proposed regulation and revise Publication 590 to the extent needed to follow that interpretation. These actions by the IRS will not affect the ability of an IRA owner to transfer funds from one IRA trustee directly to another, because such a transfer is not a rollover and, therefore, is not subject to the one rollover-per-year limitation of § 408(d)(3)(B). See Rev. Rul. 78-406, 1978-2 C.B. 157. The IRS has received comments about the administrative challenges presented by the Bobrow interpretation of § 408(d)(3)(B). The IRS understands that adoption of the Tax Court's interpretation of the statute will require IRA trustees to make changes in the processing of IRA rollovers and in IRA disclosure documents, which will take time to implement. Accordingly, the IRS will not apply the Bobrow interpretation of § 408(d)(3)(B) to any rollover that involves an IRA distribution occurring before January 1, 2015. Regardless of the ultimate resolution of the Bobrow case, the Treasury Department and the IRS expect to issue a proposed regulation under § 408 that would provide that the IRA rollover limitation applies on an aggregate basis. However, in no event would the regulation be effective before January 1, 2015.

OPTION 4: DIRECT TRANSFER TO AN IRA IN YOUR NAME

There's a word I want to use now, and it's so important that I want to put it in all caps: DIRECT. A direct rollover or transfer avoids the potholes of Direct Distribution; although it has advantages and disadvantages that you need to be aware of.

Advantages

Once you have separation of service, the IRS allows you to roll your funds directly into an IRA in your name. With a direct rollover, your retirement funds are transferred directly from your past employer's 401(k) plan to the new trustee of an IRA in your name. For example, if you decide on an asset allocation with the Well Known Fund Family, you would instruct your 401(k) administrator to make your check payable to the Well Known Fund Family, FBO (for the benefit of) your name, IRA. So if this were my check, it would read, "Well Known Fund Family, FBO David Blaydes, IRA."

This check can be mailed to you, and then you can attach it to your application and send it in. There are electronic ways to do this, but I want to use the check method to make my example easier to grasp. Since the check is technically made payable to the new trustee for your benefit instead of being made payable to you, it's not considered a distribution, so 20% is not withheld. You don't have to do anything within 60 days, and get this: There are no limitations on how many times you can use this method per year, and the same method can be used with all of your IRAs as the consolidation rule does not apply to DIRECT rollovers.

> The consolidation rule does not apply to DIRECT rollovers.

No Taxes, Penalties, or Limitations

There are no taxes, no penalties, and no limitations on how many times you can directly transfer your IRA per year.

Direct Reporting

Transferring your IRA directly does not mean you owe taxes on your 401(k) direct rollover. Most people think they should not get a 1099-R after a 401(k) rollover. The thinking is that they've rolled the money directly to another retirement account, so the IRS should not be involved. They often panic when the 1099-R arrives, because they think they'll owe income taxes.

You *will* receive a 1099-R when you do a direct 401(k) rollover, and it's not a mistake. The investment company or 401(k) fund administrator that held your money is required to send the form. The good news is if you roll the money over to another retirement account, such as an IRA, you won't have to pay any income taxes. The form is just for reporting purposes.

If you did a direct rollover, you should see the letter G in box 7 of your 1099-R. This means your company told the IRS that you did a direct rollover or transfer with your 401(k). If you do your own tax returns, you will indicate the amount of your rollover on line 15a of your 1040 income tax form when it is tax season. In 15b, you can indicate "rollover" or just put a $0 on that line.

Financial Assistance

If you work with a financial coach, they will be able to help you prepare your Financial *Life* Plan. They will help you outline your plan's necessary components: where you'll go first for cash flow, how you'll reduce your expenses, and map how to create asset allocation so you can achieve your financial goals to give you the greatest probability of success with the least amount of risk.

Investment Control and Flexibility

If you choose to directly transfer your IRA, you can invest in any IRA-approved investment. This potentially allows you to complete a well-diversified portfolio, as all asset classes are available to you. You can also choose cost-efficient, institutionally priced funds, ETFs and/or index funds, and, if you prefer, individual securities. You have almost unlimited investment choices to structure your asset allocation. I believe that control and flexibility are some of the major reasons that people opt for the direct rollover.

No Blackout Periods

If a decision to change investments is made, it is you that makes it. You can directly transfer the funds, in whole or in part, to other investments of your choice at any time without any blackout period.

Spousal Rollover

If you are a surviving spouse and receive a payment from a 401(k), you have the same rollover options that your spouse would have had. If you choose to do a rollover to an IRA, you may treat the IRA as your own or as an inherited IRA. An IRA you treat as your own is treated like any other IRA of yours, so that payment made to you before you are age 59½ will be subject to the 10% tax on early distributions and require required minimum distributions (RMDs) before you reach age 70½. If you treat the IRA as an inherited IRA, payments from the IRA will not be subject to the 10% additional income tax on distributions before age 59½. However, if your spouse had started taking RMDs, you will have to continue receiving the RMDs from the inherited IRA also. If your spouse had not started taking RMDs yet, you will not have to start receiving RMDs from the inherited IRA until the year in which your spouse would have turned age 70½.

If you are a surviving beneficiary other than a spouse, such as a child of the 401(k) participant, the only rollover option you have is to do a direct rollover to an inherited IRA. Payments from the inherited IRA will not be subject to the 10% pre–age 59½ penalty. However, you still have to take RMDs from the inherited IRA. Children or grandchildren can stretch the IRA distributions out over their life expectancy if the distributions are structured properly, thus keeping more of the IRA intact for potential future tax-deferred compounding and growth.

Let me say this a different way. If you stretch the IRA over the life expectancy of a child or grandchild, they don't have to take out very much every year and pay tax on it. They receive a lifetime of this benefit, instead of taking all the funds out on day one and paying a lot of taxes. Stretch IRAs will generate a very significant difference in the amount of total payments to the family. Stretch IRAs are a very good thing.

Income Flexibility

If you've directly transferred your IRA, then you can withdraw funds as you need them. (Just make sure you have reached the age of 59½ to avoid that 10% penalty.)

72(t) Exclusion

The 72(t) exclusion allows you, under certain circumstances, to withdraw funds from an IRA before the age of 59½ and avoid the 10% penalty. Although you cannot use the 72(t) exclusion with a 401(k), you can with an IRA. If you need funds from your retirement account and you are under the age of 59½, you would need to do a direct rollover or transfer from your 401(k) to an IRA first, then use the 72(t) exemption with your IRA. This process will eliminate the 10% penalty.

Net Unrealized Appreciation (NUA)

Even if you don't currently have stock in your 401(k), you need to read this section for two reasons. First, it can save you a lot of taxes. Second, even if you don't currently have stock in your 401(k), you might in the future. Most people have never heard of Net Unrealized Appreciation, but it can reap substantial tax savings.

If you leave a company and have significant amounts of employer stock in your 401(k) or other qualified plan, the tax law provides special optional tax benefits on your employer's stock. This stock is referred to as *Net Unrealized Appreciation* stock or *NUA shares*, because these shares have hopefully been purchased at a lower price than their current value. Consequently, the share value contains unrealized appreciation.

Using the NUA strategy, you can take a distribution of your employer's stock from their 401(k) or other qualified plans and pay ordinary income tax *only* on their basis at the time of distribution, allowing for continued tax deferral on the balance of their shares. The difference between the basis (what you paid for it way back when) and the fair market value (what it's worth) at distribution—the net unrealized appreciation—is taxed at long-term capital gains rates when the stock is eventually sold, regardless of the holding period. In other words, NUA allows you to pay tax on part of your 401(k) plan at favorable long-term capital gains rates instead of your full ordinary tax bracket. If you own company stock in your 401(k), you should be sitting on the edge of your chair. Subsequent appreciation (earned after the distribution from the qualified plan) is taxed at short- or long-term capital gains rates according to the length of the holding period, as measured from the date of the distribution. But it's only on potential gain *after* you take your distribution. Remember that long-term capital gains rates are much lower than your marginal income tax rate applied to such things as your salary and severance—about 50% less! All of that gain is taxed at favorable long-term capital gains rates, which works in your favor.

At first, it may not seem prudent to pay tax immediately on any part of your distribution when you can do a rollover and defer all taxes. However, the following has made this a lower-cost strategy:

- The large spread between the capital gains rate (15%) and the top ordinary rate (35%). You can refer to my earlier graph, check RPI's website, or Google it; long-term-capital gains rates are either 0%, 15%, and 20% for those married and filing joint taxes with incomes over $464,850 (2015). Even though 20% sounds high, that income level would put you at an ordinary income tax rate of 39.6%, so it's still 50% less.

- Large amounts of stock appreciation occurred between 1982 and 2000, 2002 to 2007, and have continued since 2009. This appreciation can benefit your funds. For example, let's assume you have tax rates of 15% for capital gains and 30% for ordinary income and that these shares did not have additional appreciation after you left your employer. Over the years, you opted to have some of your 401(k) contributions invested in shares of your employer's stock at a total of $10,000. Those shares are now worth $100,000. Your options are to have the stock distributed to you when you leave the company and pay tax on the basis (the $10,000 invested) or, alternatively, to roll over all of the shares into your IRA and pay tax later, possibly decades later.

Following is the difference in your options:

○ Take stock and pay ordinary tax now (30%) on the $10,000 basis and on the appreciation later with a capital gains rate (15%) for a total tax $16,500.

○ Roll over the shares to your IRA and pay tax at ordinary rates (30%) later, for a total tax of $30,000.

You save almost half of the tax by using the net unrealized appreciation rules. Note that you may opt to use NUA treatment for only some of your employer's shares and roll over the rest.

To take advantage of the NUA option, you must elect a lump sum, in-kind distribution from the plan of your stock (a complete distribution of all plan assets in a single calendar year). If you have mutual funds in addition to the company stock, you can take the stock as a distribution to qualify for the special tax treatment of the stock, while rolling the mutual funds over into an IRA to avoid taxation on the funds. A *lump sum distribution* is defined as distribution or payment within one taxable year of the recipient of the balance to the credit of an employee, which becomes payable to the recipient on account of the employee's death, after the employee attains age 59½, on account of the employee's separation from service, or after the employee has become disabled.

In my experience, when a person leaves a company, they make some financial decisions and contact us after the fact. In reviewing their situation, we find that they did a direct rollover of their 401(k) mutual funds into an IRA last year and kept their company stock in the 401(k). We then determine the stock has a tremendous gain and would have recommended the individual utilize the NUA technique to withdraw the stock, pay taxes on the cost basis only, then sell the stock the following day at long-term capital gains rates to diversify. They would then be able to pay the more tax-favorable long-term capital gains rates on the appreciation of their company stock, even though it was in a 401(k). However, because the individual did a rollover with their 401(k) mutual funds last year, they are no longer eligible for the tax saving NUA technique, because they did not meet the complete distribution in the same tax year. Ouch!

Another example of someone contacting us after the fact is when an individual transfers their entire 401(k) into an IRA first, then they come to us for a Financial *Life* Plan to determine how to best allocate their IRA funds. The company stock that they rolled over with their mutual funds had a substantial increase in value and was rolled over into a personal IRA. Because the rollover was done on a direct basis, no withholding tax was paid. However, since the stock had already been rolled over, they were no longer eligible for the tax savings they could have benefitted from using the NUA technique. Now do you understand why I stress having a Financial *Life* Plan done *before* making any financial decisions?

In another example, we held a meeting with someone who had already done a direct transfer with their 401(k) plan into a variety of investments with a broker that a friend had referred to them. The transfer was emotionally driven, as they were very upset with their previous employer for firing them. However, we found that their previous 401(k) plan had a great number of low-cost investment options with an administrator that offered asset allocation assistance at no cost. Although they did not offer a Financial *Life* Plan, the administrator offered a risk tolerance questionnaire that assisted the 401(k) administrator with at least helping the individual with a decent asset allocation of the their funds. The bottom line is they should have never transferred their 401(k).

Keep in mind that the use of the NUA option does not require that you use it for all employer shares. You may have 10,000 shares of your employer's stock, and you can decide to roll over 5,000 shares and avoid current taxation and then pay tax on the other 5,000 shares, per the NUA rules. To maximize such a division, you want to obtain the cost basis of various lots of their stock from your plan administrator and review them to determine which shares might benefit most from the special NUA tax treatment. For example, it might make sense to use the NUA strategy on shares with the lowest cost basis relative to fair market value at distribution (and thus the greatest amount of NUA), and roll over shares with a *higher* cost basis, relative to the fair market value at distribution.

Currently, the capital gains rate is scheduled to drop to 0% for those in the 15% tax bracket and below. Therefore, qualifying workers can retire during a period when the capital gains rate can be 0% and get a huge tax advantage. Not everyone will qualify, but now is the time to see a financial coach and find out, not after you potentially do something that makes you ineligible to use the NUA technique.

Disadvantages

Now that we have covered many of the advantages of a direct rollover, let's discuss the disadvantages:

Required Minimum Distributions (RMD)

Funds transferred into an IRA are subject to RMD requirements. When you turn 70½, you have to start taking taxable distributions of approximately 3.65% of your total funds in the first year, even if you are still working. However, at 70½, let's make sure your Financial *Life* Plan results in you being too busy spending time with grandchildren, playing golf, and traveling to work!

Fees and Expenses

Be wary of "free" or "no fee" claims. Competition among brokerage firms for IRA rollover business is strong; therefore, advertising about rollovers and IRA-related services is common. This advertising can be misleading if it implies there are not fees charged to investors who have accounts with their firm. Even if there are not costs associated with the rollover itself, there will almost certainly be costs related to account management. Before making a decision to directly roll over your 401(k), you should check the fees and expenses related to the investments you are rolling your money to. I strongly believe in investing in the most cost-efficient manner possible, as long as you do not sacrifice something meaningful in the process. As an example, I like the cost efficiencies inherit with ETF and index funds especially for growth-oriented portfolios. However, for defensive portfolios, passive ETF and index funds will potentially not have the same downside protection that a managed volatility manager will have. As a disclosure, just because a manager might be attempting to manage your volatility, there's no guarantee they will be successful. On the subject of fees, if you are working with a broker or a financial coach, you need to make sure you are fully informed of any and all fees. I am a strong supporter of complete transparency and full disclosure.

A few years ago I had my eyes examined at a large "big box" eyeglass store. Following my eye exam, the optometrist told me what prescription I needed and then walked me out and personally introduced me to an eyeglass salesperson. The fact that the doctor was walking me out to a waiting salesperson was overly obvious, so I politely asked the optometrist if he received compensation, directly or indirectly, on the glasses I purchased. I thought he was going to pass out at my question, and his stammering and stuttering provided my answer. I didn't like this. Don't misunderstand me. I don't mind the optometrist receiving compensation for the referral (as long as I really did need glasses). I just didn't like the lack of transparency. I feel so strongly about transparency in my business that I expected it to carry over to the big box eyeglass store. In any event, I left. I don't want to work with anyone who does not provide conflict-free full disclosure and complete transparency, and I encourage you to feel the same way, especially when it comes to your investments.

Loans
Unlike a 401(k), loans are not available with IRAs.

Creditors
Although IRAs are protected in bankruptcy proceedings, state laws vary on whether IRA assets are protected in lawsuits. I prefer those in high-liability professions, such as anesthesiologists or medical practitioners, remain in ERISA type retirement plans because they remain better protected.

Conflicts of Interest
If you are working with a broker or other investment professional, they may have a conflict of interest at the company they work at. The company may mandate the broker recommend only the investments they dictate. This is one of the main reasons I suggest you work with only transparent, independent advisors who are working for *you*, instead of their brokerage company. Even in this case, a conflict of interest could exist, because the advisor potentially receives an investment advisory fee if you roll your 401(k) into an IRA, and they may not receive the advisory fee if you kept your funds in the 401(k). I'm not saying being compensated for work performed in your behalf is bad; I'm just saying you should be aware of it, so you can make an informed

decision. I am a firm believer in full disclosure and complete transparency, and you should be too!

> I am a very firm believer in full disclosure and complete transparency, and you should be too!

While we're on the subject of working with an advisor, I want to point out FINRA's Rule 2111, known as their *suitability rule*. I feel strongly that anyone who is going to give you financial or investment advice should follow this rule.

FINRA Rule 2111 rightfully requires that an investment advisor have a reasonable basis to believe that a recommended transaction or investment strategy involving a security or investment is suitable for their client. A firm and its registered representatives, before making a recommendation, must consider your investment profile and a variety of factors. These include your age, other investments, financial situation and needs, tax status, investment objectives, investment experience, investment time horizon, liquidity needs, risk tolerance, and any other information the firm would need to form a basis for their recommendation. If the investment advisor you are working with does not ask the questions necessary to obtain this information, be very hesitant to take their advice.

401(K) LOANS

If you've taken a loan against your 401(k) and then find yourself separated from service, you need to find out how your employer is going to handle your loan. Many times your old employer will deem your loan balance a distribution if you do not repay it within 90 days. This action results in full taxation of the loan balance and an additional 10% penalty if you are under the age of 59½. If this is the case with your loan, look back at the earlier chapter that dealt with cash flow and see if any of those sources will produce enough money to pay off all or some of your loan. Some companies will allow you to continue making loan payments, but only if you leave the funds with them. Wouldn't this be nice to know before you make a decision to take a direct distribution or a direct rollover? I bring this up because very few individuals know their loan will become taxable in 90 days and don't plan ahead for the taxes that will be due on that loan next April 15.

457(B) PLANS

I want to mention something unique for you in the event you have a 457(b) plan instead of a 401(k). If the plan is a governmental section 457(b) plan, the same rules apply as a 401(k), with one difference. If you do not do a rollover, you will not have to pay the 10% pre–age 59½ tax.

ROTH IRAS

We get a lot of questions concerning converting IRAs into a Roth, so I want to spend a couple of minutes on this before we drive away from this chapter. If you roll over a payment from your 401(k) to a Roth IRA, a special rule applies that will tax the amount of the payment rollover. However, the 10% additional income tax on early distributions will not apply unless you take the rollover out of the Roth IRA within five years, counting from January 1 of the year of the rollover. If you roll over the payment to a Roth IRA, later payments from the Roth IRA that are qualified distributions will not be taxed. A qualified distribution from a Roth IRA is a payment made after you reach age 59½ and after you have had the Roth IRA for at least five years. In applying this five-year rule, you count from January 1 of the year for which your first contribution was made to the Roth IRA; you do not have to take a required minimum distribution from a Roth IRA at age 70½ like you have to do from regular IRAs. So why would you consider doing a Roth conversion now and paying income tax on 100% on the amount converted? Typically you would only do this if you expect to be in a higher income tax bracket after age 70½, and you do not want to be forced to take RMDs at that time. Clients who have substantial deferred compensation plans that will start to pay out at age 70 generally prefer this plan.

So, we've covered the four primary options with your former company's retirement plan. Exhibit 1 summarizes the pros and cons of each decision.

PRIMARY OPTIONS WITH RETIREMENT ACCOUNTS–PROS AND CONS

	Keep In Former Employer's Plan	Rollover to New Employer's Plan	Take a Taxable Distribution	Direct Rollover
PROS	Easy Fees may be less Age 55 penalty free w/d Possible advice Company stock Creditor Protection	Consolidation Company stock No RMDs Possible loans	60 day assess	No taxes No penalties Direct IRS reporting Financial assistance Unlimited investments No blackout periods Spousal rollovers Stretch for children Income flexibility 72(t) allowed NUA allowed
CONS	Limited investments Limited or no advice No consolidation Blackout periods Cannot 72(t) Cannot Roth convert Negative emotions	Limited investments Limited or no advice No consolidation Blackout periods Cannot 72(t) Cannot Roth convert Negative emotions	20% withheld 20% up out of savings Possibly taxed Pre 59½, 10% penalty 1 rollover per year All IRA's consolidated	RMD's required Fees and expenses No loans Less creditor protection Possible conflicts of interest Suitability

Exhibit 1: The Pros and Cons of Retirement Account Options

Your 401(k) is probably your largest investment, so it's important to protect it from potential taxes and penalties that can take you off the road toward your future financial goals. The four options you have with your 401(k) all have pros and cons. There is no one answer. After you complete your Financial *Life* Plan and review your investment allocation, what you should do with your 401(k) will become more evident. You have options that, when done right, don't have to cost you a dime in taxes or penalties. And it's nice to have options!

> **It's nice to have options!**

CHAPTER 5

SETTING YOUR
FINANCIAL GPS: THE 91.5% ASSET
ALLOCATION FACTOR

 **HOW ARE YOU GOING** to know if you are on the right path financially? How can you put these financial stressors behind you so that you can focus on your job search? If you get two job offers, one with better income and the other better benefits, which of the two should you take?

When I travel, I typically set my in-dash GPS, so I can focus on other things while I'm driving. The GPS allows me to make calls or visit with a passenger as a quick glance to the dash tells me whether I'm on my route or not. A Financial *Life* Plan does the same thing; except instead of it allowing you to make calls, it allows you to focus on your job search or transition into retirement.

So how do you add a GPS to your Financial *Life* Plan? How do you know what direction you should take for the many decisions you face? How do you know what percent you should have in stocks and how much in bonds? What about the different classes of stocks, such as domestic and international, large company and small company, growth oriented vs. value? We call this *asset allocation*. Asset allocation is similar to a recipe; it's like knowing how much of each ingredient to put into your financial batter.

A few years ago, my daughter, Lauren, baked a batch of my favorite cookies for my birthday—Oatmeal Scotches. They came out of the oven as thin as a sheet of paper. I said, "Lo, you must have made a mistake with the ingredients. Perhaps you put in too many eggs and too much butter and not enough flour."

She admitted she skipped the vanilla extract because of how bad it tasted. I explained that although vanilla extract tastes terrible by itself, if the right amount is added to the batter, the cookies taste better. The same idea holds true with the asset allocation of your investments. Like the ingredients in the batter, having too much or too little of an asset class, even the bad tasting ones like emerging market equities and high-yield (junk) bonds, will do more harm than good if that's all you put in your portfolio. When the right amount of each is added, the overall result is a less volatile portfolio.

Asset allocation relies on the notions that different asset classes offer returns that are not perfectly correlated and diversifying portfolios across asset classes will potentially help to reduce volatility and optimize risk-adjusted returns. Asset allocation went largely unexplored until 1986, when Gary Brinson, CFA, a Chicago-based pension consulting firm, Randolph

Hood, and Gilbert L. Beebower of SEI Investments in Oaks, Pennsylvania, (known collectively as BHB) sought to explain the effects of asset allocation on pension plan returns. In their paper, "Determinants of Portfolio Performance," published in the *Financial Analysts Journal*,[8] BHB stated that asset allocation is the primary determinant of a portfolio's return variability, with security selection and market timing playing minor roles. BHB's 1986 study examined the quarterly returns of 91 large US pension funds over the 1974 to 1983 period. BHB concluded that asset allocation was responsible for 93.6% of the *variation* in a portfolio's quarterly returns.

In 1991 Brinson, Hood, and Brian D. Singer published an update to the BHB study that examined returns from 1977 to 1987. They found a return variance of 91.5%, essentially confirming the results of the original study,[9] which remains the foundation for asset allocation today.

The BHB study was focused only on the *variability* of returns and not on return levels or relative performance. In 2000, Ibbotson and Paul D. Kaplan addressed these misconceptions in "Does Asset Allocation Policy Explain 40, 90 or 100 Percent of Performance?" The authors looked at 10 years of monthly returns for 94 balanced mutual funds and 10 years of quarterly returns for 58 pension funds and confirmed the BHB results.

---

8   David Larrabe, "Setting the Record Straight on Asset Allocation," CFA Institute, February 16 2012.

9   Gary P. Brinson, Brian D. Singer, and Gilbert L. Beebower, "Determinants of Portfolio Performance II: An Update," *Financial Analysts Journal*, 1991.

They found that asset allocation did indeed explain about 90% of the period-to-period variability of a portfolio.[10]

Today this study is widely known as the Brinson Beebower study, and it is used as the foundation for large institutional pension plans and individual portfolios such as yours.

So how important is having the right mix, or asset allocation, when it comes to the returns of a portfolio? As Exhibit 2 shows, very!

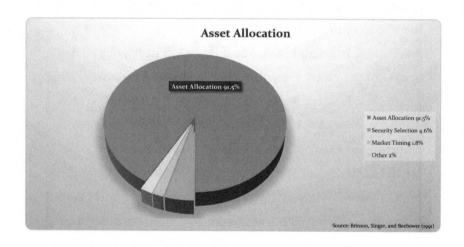

Exhibit 2: Asset Allocation © SEI

That's right! Proper asset allocation drives 91.5% of the return. Picking the right investment, such as the hot fund of last year (chasing returns), accounts for only 4.6% of the return.

---

10   Roger G. Ibbotson and Paul D. Kaplan, "Does Asset Allocation Policy Explain 40, 90, 100 Percent of Performance?" *Financial Analysts Journal 56*, no 1, (2000).

Let me use Exhibit 3 to support why "chasing" returns does not work. How many times have you heard or read an analyst say, "Past performance does not guarantee future results."

This message is repeated inside every marketing piece about investment that mentions performance, because it is true. Looking at listings of managers ranked by their three-, five-, or ten-year returns provides little insight into future performance. Many investors learn about the latest hot fund or stock and sell their current holdings to buy what's hot. But trying to predict future performance based on past results isn't a consistently reliable method of investing. You may end up selling when you should be buying, and vice versa. Here's how investment decisions based on past performance alone can be a mistake.

Investors can actually hurt their chances for attractive returns by chasing hot investments. Yesterday's top performer could be tomorrow's laggard. Exhibit 3 follows the performance of all of the large-cap value funds in the Morningstar Large Cap Value category for two consecutive five-year periods, 2006–2010 and 2011–2015. Of the funds that ranked in the top 25% of the group in the first period, more than 50% dropped to the bottom two quartiles, or completely out of existence during the second. Ranking managers by their five-year return provides little insight into future performance.

42% of the top quartile managers from 2011–2015 did not have a full five-year track record during the previous period.[11]

---

11 SEI, Morningstar Direct, "US Large Blend Universe over the entire 10-year period from 12/31/2005 through 12/31/2015." 2015.

Past Performance Does Not Guarantee Future Results

This message is repeated on every investment marketing piece that mentions performance—because it is true. Looking at listings of managers ranked by their three-, five- or 10-year returns provides little insight into future performance. Many investors learn about the latest "hot" fund or stock and sell their current holdings to buy what's "hot." But trying to predict future performance based on past results isn't a consistently reliable method of investing. You may end up selling when you should be buying, and vice versa. Here's how investment decisions based on past performance alone can be a mistake.

Investors can actually hurt their chances for attractive returns by chasing "hot" investments. Yesterday's top performer could be tomorrow's laggard.

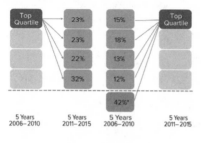

The chart follows the performance of all of the large-cap value funds in the Morningstar Large Cap Value category for two consecutive five-year periods—2006 through 2010 and then 2011 through 2015. Of the funds that ranked in the top 25% of the group in the first period, more than 50% dropped to the bottom quartiles—or completely out of existence. Ranking managers by their five-year returns provides little insight into future performance.

*42% of the top quartile managers from 2011-2015 did not have a full five-year track record during the previous period

Source: SEI, Morningstar Direct, U.S. Large Blend Universe over the entire 10-year period from 12/31/05 through 12/31/15.

Based on the Morningstar universe of 4,125 U.S. Equity Large Cap Blend managers.

Exhibit 3: Past Performance © SEI

As you can see, chasing the hot return of the recent past does not work, yet this is how many decide what to invest their life savings in.

Let's not even talk about market timing, since you would have to be correct twice: when to get out and when to get back in. And, as we saw on the previous exhibit, it provides less than 2% to the overall success anyway.

In Exhibit 4 using the S&P 500 as a proxy for the domestic equity market and looking at a 20-year investment period between 1/1/1995 and 12/31/2014 (or 5,036 trading days), marketing timing seemed to indicate—

- If you missed just the 10 best trading days, your return would drop from 9.85% annually to 4.49%.

- If you missed the 20 best trading days, your return dropped from 9.85% to 2.05%.

- If you missed the 40 best trading days, your return dropped from 9.85% to -1.96%, a loss.

Just missing the best 40 out of 5,036 trading days meant a loss instead of a 9.85% average annual return. Now do you start to understand why you are always hearing, "You can't time the market?"

Mistakes That Can Hurt Investors

The Risks of Timing the Market

Although the financial markets can be remarkably steady over longer time periods, sharp short-term movements in security prices are increasingly frequent. As individual investors witness the market making big point swings, they are often drawn to try "timing" the market — attempting to buy or sell based on the direction the market may be headed. Choosing the "ideal moment" to buy or sell is difficult and, as you can see below, investors who attempt to time the market may end up missing periods of exceptional returns.

Two Potential Keys to Success: Patience and Commitment
Average Annual Total Return: (1/1/1995-12/31/2014)

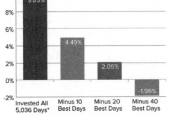

Using the S&P 500 as a proxy for the domestic equity market, and looking at a 20-year investment period, we see that:

- If an investor missed just the 10 best days, 63% of the gains would be lost.
- If they missed the 20 best days, about 87% of the gains are gone.
- Missing 40 best days resulted in an even more significant loss.

While volatility can provide the opportunity to buy stocks and mutual funds at attractive prices, market timing can seriously diminish long-term performance.

Past performance is no guarantee of future results. The investment return and principal value of an investment will fluctuate.

Source: Goldman Sachs Asset Management. Calculation is based on 5,036 days, excluding weekends and holidays. The returns are based on the S&P 500 Index, a market-weighted index of 500 of the largest U.S. stocks in a variety of industry sectors. It is not possible to invest directly in an unmanaged index. Equity securities are more volatile than bonds and subject to greater risks. Small and mid-sized company stocks involve greater risks than those customarily associated with larger companies.

This material is provided for educational purposes only and should not be construed as investment advice or an offer or solicitation to buy or sell securities. Opinions expressed are current opinions as of the date appearing in this material only.

Exhibit 4: Trying to Time the Market © SEI

Callan charts, the standard for investment-oriented charts, show how all the different asset classes come in and out of favor over time. If you invested in last year's hot fund, it may not be due to the managers of that fund being smarter than anyone else. It's more likely they were in the right asset class at the right time. If you chase last year's hot return and invest heavily in that fund/asset class, as the chart indicates, you may very well find yourself toward the bottom of the chart the following year. Since it's impossible to know which asset classes are going to do well in the future (unless you have a crystal ball), the smartest thing to do is to diversify and invest the right amount in different asset classes, so that you're spreading your risk. Now this doesn't mean you should invest an equal amount in each asset class.

> Now this doesn't mean you should invest an equal amount in each asset class.

Some asset classes are riskier than others, and therefore should have a lessor amount. When we baked our cookies, you'll recall we didn't put an equal amount of vanilla extract in the batter as brown sugar. An equal amount of vanilla extract would do to the cookies what potentially an equal amount of higher-risk small cap growth equities would do to your risk.

Take a look at Exhibit 5. If you were sitting at the end of 2007, wouldn't it be tempting to chase the performance that you had seen recently in International funds? After all, that asset class did great the previous year. If you gave into that temptation of chasing performance, you would not be very happy the next year, when that asset class went to the bottom! Likewise, would it not have been tempting to get out of International funds at the end of 2011, after they ended up at the bottom of the heap? You would have regretted that in 2012, when that same asset class raced back to the top.

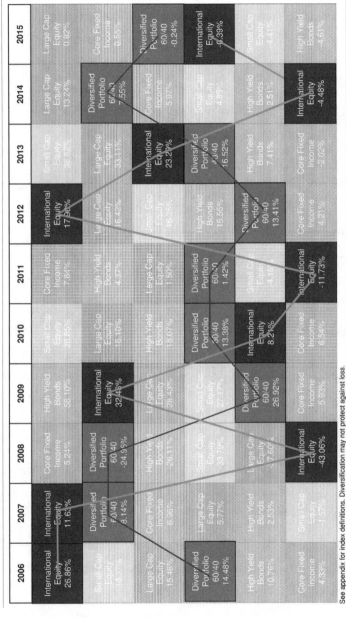

Asset Class Returns

	2006	2007	2008	2009	2010	2011	2012	2013	2014	2015
	International Equity 26.86%	International Equity 11.63%	Core Fixed Income 5.24%	High Yield Bonds 58.10%	Small Cap Equity 26.85%	Core Fixed Income 7.84%	International Equity 17.90%	Small Cap Equity 38.82%	Large Cap Equity 13.24%	Large Cap Equity 0.92%
	Small Cap Equity 18.37%	Diversified Portfolio 60/40 8.14%	Diversified Portfolio 60/40 -24.95%	International Equity 32.46%	Large Cap Equity 16.10%	High Yield Bonds 4.37%	Large Cap Equity 16.42%	Large Cap Equity 33.11%	Diversified Portfolio 60/40 7.55%	Core Fixed Income -0.55%
	Large Cap Equity 15.46%	Core Fixed Income 6.96%	High Yield Bonds -26.11%	Large Cap Equity 28.43%	High Yield Bonds 15.07%	Large Cap Equity 1.50%	Small Cap Equity 16.35%	International Equity 23.29%	Core Fixed Income 5.97%	Diversified Portfolio 60/40 -0.24%
	Diversified Portfolio 60/40 14.48%	Large Cap Equity 5.77%	Small Cap Equity -33.79%	Small Cap Equity 27.17%	Diversified Portfolio 30/40 13.38%	Diversified Portfolio 60/40 1.42%	High Yield Bonds 15.55%	Diversified Portfolio 60/40 16.52%	Small Cap Equity 4.89%	International Equity -0.39%
	High Yield Bonds 10.76%	High Yield Bonds 2.53%	Large Cap Equity -37.60%	Diversified Portfolio 60/40 26.92%	International Equity 8.21%	Small Cap Equity -4.18%	Diversified Portfolio 60/40 13.41%	High Yield Bonds 7.41%	High Yield Bonds 2.51%	Small Cap Equity -4.41%
	Core Fixed Income 4.33%	Small Cap Equity -1.57%	International Equity -43.06%	Core Fixed Income 5.93%	Core Fixed Income 6.54%	International Equity -11.73%	Core Fixed Income -4.21%	Core Fixed Income -2.02%	International Equity -4.48%	High Yield Bonds -4.61%

See appendix for index definitions. Diversification may not protect against loss.

Source: FactSet. Not intended to represent the performance of any particular investment.
Indices are unmanaged and one cannot invest directly in an index. For financial intermediary use only. Not for public distribution.
Past performance is no guarantee of future returns.

SEI New ways.
New answers.*

Exhibit 5: Asset Class Returns for International Funds © SEI

67

Let's look at another example: Exhibit 6 includes the equities of small companies, something we refer to as *small cap*. If you were to chase the performance of this asset class at the end of 2010, you would not have been happy with that decision the following year. The same would hold true if you decided to sell out after it performed poorly in a down year, only to see it rebound the next year.

The problem here is that most people aren't even aware they are chasing returns when they decide to bail out of a mutual fund due to its poor recent performance. They might think it's just a bad fund versus a good fund when it might just be an asset class that is temporarily out of favor.

Now you know the secret to making good-tasting cookies is following the recipe with the right amount of each ingredient, and the secret to having the right portfolio that will give you the highest probability of success with no more risk than necessary is matching the allocation to what your Financial *Life* Plan dictates.

We just learned that 91.5% of investment returns are derived by how you allocate your investments. Allocation doesn't mean you invest all of your funds in several mutual funds that buy the stocks of large-cap growth companies, because no matter how many large-cap growth funds you buy, you would still only own one asset class. The asset allocation of your portfolio should be across many asset classes that are not correlated with each other on a one-to-one basis. In other words, you want to have some asset classes that will hopefully go up when the others

Asset Class Returns

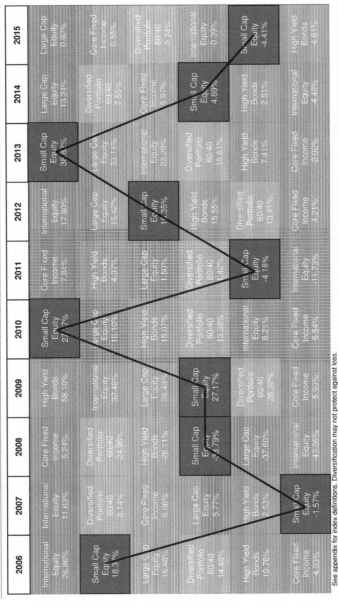

2006	2007	2008	2009	2010	2011	2012	2013	2014	2015
International Equity 26.86%	International Equity 11.63%	Core Fixed Income 5.24%	High Yield Bonds 58.10%	Small Cap Equity 27.7%	Core Fixed Income 7.84%	International Equity 17.90%	Small Cap Equity 38.82%	Large Cap Equity 13.24%	Large Cap Equity 0.92%
Small Cap Equity 18.37%	Diversified Portfolio 60/40 8.14%	Diversified Portfolio 60/40 -24.96%	International Equity 32.46%	Large Cap Equity 16.10%	High Yield Bonds 4.37%	Large Cap Equity 15.42%	Large Cap Equity 33.11%	Diversified Portfolio 60/40 7.55%	Core Fixed Income 0.58%
Large Cap Equity 15.46%	Core Fixed Income 6.96%	High Yield Bonds -26.11%	Large Cap Equity 28.43%	High Yield Bonds 15.07%	Large Cap Equity 1.50%	Small Cap Equity 17.35%	International Equity 23.29%	Core Fixed Income 5.97%	Diversified Portfolio 60/40 0.24%
Diversified Portfolio 60/40 14.48%	Large Cap Equity 5.77%	Small Cap Equity -33.79%	Small Cap Equity 27.17%	Diversified Portfolio 60/40 13.38%	Diversified Portfolio 60/40 0.42%	High Yield Bonds 15.55%	Diversified Portfolio 60/40 15.61%	Small Cap Equity 4.89%	International Equity -0.39%
High Yield Bonds 10.76%	High Yield Bonds 2.53%	Large Cap Equity -37.60%	Diversified Portfolio 60/40 26.92%	International Equity 8.21%	Small Cap Equity -4.18%	Diversified Portfolio 60/40 13.41%	High Yield Bonds 7.41%	High Yield Bonds 2.51%	Small Cap Equity -4.41%
Core Fixed Income -4.33%	Small Cap Equity -1.57%	International Equity -43.06%	Core Fixed Income 5.93%	Core Fixed Income 6.54%	International Equity -11.73%	Core Fixed Income 4.21%	Core Fixed Income -2.02%	International Equity -4.48%	High Yield Bonds -4.61%

See appendix for index definitions. Diversification may not protect against loss.

SEI New ways. New answers.®

Source: FactSet. Not intended to represent the performance of any particular investment. Indices are unmanaged and one cannot invest directly in an index. For financial intermediary use only. Not for public distribution. Past performance is no guarantee of future returns.

68

Exhibit 6: Asset Class Returns for Small Cap Equity © SEI

go down. Examples of asset classes include, but are not limited to, large-cap growth, large-cap value, mid-cap growth, mid-cap value, small-cap growth, small-cap value, International, Emerging market equities, Investment-grade bonds, high-yield bonds, and emerging market bonds.

In a few chapters, I'll show you how to determine the best allocation for your personal situation, the one that will give you the highest probability of success with no more risk than is necessary. For now, I want to continue to discuss the basics. Exhibit 7 shows the rate of return (ROR) for various asset classes over the last fifteen years. Do you see how a diversified portfolio fell to the middle? In other words, proper diversification can help take the highs and lows out of your volatility.

OVERLAYING YOUR LIFE ONTO INVESTMENT RESEARCH AND ANALYSIS

At RPI, our investment philosophy is focused on meeting clients' objectives and managing their risk. This tailored approach to the development of investment strategy has evolved so that our clients' portfolios can be positioned to take advantage of market inefficiencies and the attractive opportunities they present.

Asset Class Returns

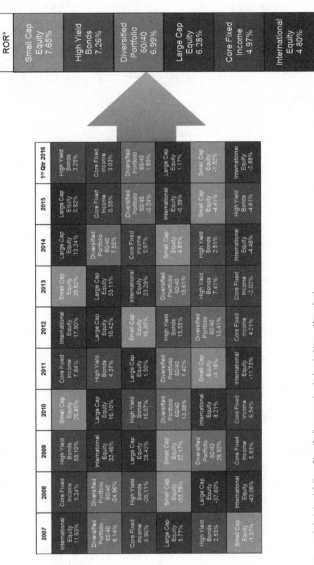

2007	2008	2009	2010	2011	2012	2013	2014	2015	1st Qtr 2016
International Equity 11.63%	Core Fixed Income 5.24%	High Yield Bonds 58.10%	Small Cap Equity 26.85%	Core Fixed Income 7.84%	International Equity 17.90%	Small Cap Equity 38.82%	Large Cap Equity 13.24%	Large Cap Equity 0.92%	High Yield Bonds 3.25%
Diversified Portfolio 60/40 8.14%	Diversified Portfolio 60/40 -24.96%	International Equity 32.46%	Large Cap Equity 16.10%	High Yield Bonds 4.37%	Large Cap Equity 16.42%	Large Cap Equity 33.11%	Diversified Portfolio 60/40 7.55%	Core Fixed Income 0.55%	Core Fixed Income 3.03%
Core Fixed Income 6.96%	High Yield Bonds -26.11%	Large Cap Equity 28.43%	High Yield Bonds 15.07%	Large Cap Equity 1.50%	Small Cap Equity 16.35%	International Equity 23.29%	Core Fixed Income 5.97%	Diversified Portfolio 60/40 -0.24%	Diversified Portfolio 60/40 1.89%
Large Cap Equity 5.77%	Small Cap Equity -33.79%	Small Cap Equity 27.17%	Diversified Portfolio 60/40 13.38%	Diversified Portfolio 60/40 1.42%	High Yield Bonds 15.55%	Diversified Portfolio 60/40 15.61%	Small Cap Equity 4.89%	International Equity -0.39%	Large Cap Equity 1.17%
High Yield Bonds 2.53%	Large Cap Equity -37.60%	Diversified Portfolio 60/40 26.92%	International Equity 8.21%	Small Cap Equity -4.18%	Diversified Portfolio 60/40 13.41%	High Yield Bonds 7.41%	High Yield Bonds 2.51%	Small Cap Equity -4.41%	Small Cap Equity -1.52%
Small Cap Equity -1.57%	International Equity -43.06%	Core Fixed Income 5.93%	Core Fixed Income 6.54%	International Equity -11.73%	Core Fixed Income 4.21%	Core Fixed Income -2.02%	International Equity -4.48%	High Yield Bonds -4.61%	International Equity -2.88%

15 Year ROR*
Small Cap Equity 7.65%
High Yield Bonds 7.26%
Diversified Portfolio 60/40 6.99%
Large Cap Equity 6.28%
Core Fixed Income 4.97%
International Equity 4.80%

See appendix for index definitions. Diversification may not protect against loss.   *Annualized

Source: *FactSet.* Not intended to represent the performance of any particular investment. Indices are unmanaged and one cannot invest directly in an index. For financial intermediary use only. Not for public distribution. Past performance is no guarantee of future returns.

SEI   New ways. New answers.®

68

Exhibit 7: The Benefits of Diversification © SEI

The most important part of our approach is understanding our clients and their needs. Only then can we begin building an investor's particular investment strategy. At RPI, we believe the comprehensive approach to discovery and assessment can be one of the most critical conversations we have with our clients. In this conversation, some questions need to be thoroughly explored, specifically—

- What are your goals and objectives? Near-term? Long-term? What is mandatory?

- What are the risks to be guarded against in the process? What are the consequences of guarding against these risks and dealing with them?

Only when these questions have been fully discussed and defined can the investment process begin. We work to initiate an investment process based on the following principles:

- **Asset Allocation:** We create strategies with appropriate diversification among asset classes and between investment approaches, which are crucial drivers of investment success.

- **Portfolio Design:** We identify alpha sources, or returns in excess of benchmark returns, across our equity, fixed-income, and alternative investment portfolios.

- **Investment Manager Selection:** We evaluate our clients' individual holdings and monitor their managers' performance.

- **Portfolio Construction and Management:** We use investments with complementary objectives to ensure diversification of risk and return within portfolios.

- **Tax Management:** We help investors keep more of what they earn through year-round efforts to reduce tax obligations.

- **Risk Management:** We oversee each manager's investment approach, making sure the approach aligns with the objectives of the portfolio segments.

Read on to learn how you'll decide how much you should invest in each asset class.

CHAPTER 6

KEEPING RIGHT: HOW

TO REVIEW YOUR PORTFOLIO

IN THE PREVIOUS CHAPTER, we talked about how to optimize your return and reduce volatility by investing in different asset classes. Many people feel that the more aggressively they invest, the greater their potential of achieving greater returns with an increased probability of financial success. Although that may be true in some cases, it also increases the risks! We typically refer to volatility or risk as *standard deviation*. Understanding standard deviation is going to be critical as we proceed with this chapter.

With dealing with investments, standard deviation is used to determine how much a return will vary from its expected return. This gives you an idea how much the returns will vary, up or down, so that you can compare the volatility of the investment to such things as your risk tolerance.

Let me put this in terms we can all better understand. Let's say you are in a portfolio with an average rate of return of 10% with a standard deviation of 4. This means that 68% of the time, the fund will return between 6% and 14%, or it's 10% average plus or minus its standard deviation of 4. The 68% is known as one standard deviation.

Two standard deviations give us a likelihood that 95% of the time the 10% average return will vary another 4%, so now we are at 2% and 18%. Three standard deviations give us a likelihood that 98% of the time the 10% average return will vary another 4%, so now we are at a -2% and 22%.

Here is why standard deviation is so important. Our portfolios have an investment policy statement (IPS) that provides the different standard deviations, so before you ever invest, you can know what the worst and best case scenarios are 95% or 98% of the time. If the down number represents a percentage loss where you know you'd be looking for a window to jump out of if that happened to your portfolio, then you know its allocation is too aggressive for you. Wouldn't it be nice to know this potential before you invested and before you suffered a loss outside of your risk tolerance or comfort zone?

Now that we understand standard deviation, let's look at Exhibit 8. This chart shows the potential relationship between the percentage that is in stocks versus bonds against the standard deviation and how it correlates to the worst one-year loss.

Portfolio Table

The Risk-Based Portfolio was selected from this list of Portfolios, based upon the risk assessment. The Target Band is comprised of the portfolio(s) that could be appropriate for you, based upon the Risk-Based Portfolio indicated. The Target Portfolio was selected by you. The Average Real Return is equal to the Average Total Return minus the inflation rate of 4.07%. Refer to the Worst 1-Year Loss and Standard Deviation columns in the chart below to compare the relative risks of your Current Portfolio to the Target Portfolio.

Current	Risk Based	Target Band	Name	Cash	Bond	Stock	Alternative	Average Return		Worst 1 Year Loss	Standard Deviation
								Total	Real		
	↑		Capital Preservation I	5%	67%	28%	0%	7.61%	3.54%	-4.97%	5.90%
↑			Current	38%	15%	47%	0%	7.83%	3.76%	-16.21%	8.25%
		↑	Capital Preservation II	5%	57%	38%	0%	7.98%	3.91%	-9.56%	7.12%
		↑	Balanced I	4%	51%	45%	0%	8.25%	4.18%	-12.65%	8.11%
			Balanced II	4%	42%	54%	0%	8.56%	4.49%	-16.97%	9.43%
			Total Return I	4%	35%	61%	0%	8.79%	4.72%	-20.80%	10.54%
			Total Return II	3%	25%	72%	0%	9.18%	5.11%	-26.07%	12.34%
			Capital Growth I	2%	16%	82%	0%	9.63%	5.56%	-30.63%	14.04%
			Capital Growth II	0%	9%	91%	0%	9.92%	5.85%	-35.12%	15.56%
			Equity Growth	0%	0%	100%	0%	10.22%	6.15%	-39.57%	17.12%

Return vs. Risk Graph

When deciding how to invest your money, you must determine the amount of risk you are willing to assume to pursue a desired return. The Return versus Risk Graph reflects a set of portfolios that assume a low relative level of risk for each level of return, or conversely an optimal return for the degree of investment risk taken. The graph also shows the position of the Current, Target, Risk-Based, and Custom Portfolios. The positioning of these portfolios illustrates how their respective risks and returns compare to each other as well as the optimized level of risk and return represented by the Portfolios.

This graph shows the relationship of return and risk for each Portfolio in the chart above.

Exhibit 8: Returns, Risk and Standard Deviation©PIEtech, Inc.

As shown in Exhibit 8, the equity growth portfolio is invested 100% in equities or stocks that historically averaged an annual return of 10.22%. Now take a look at the total return I portfolio, which has only 61% invested in stocks with a historical annual return of 8.79%. This is approximately 1% less. So then we invest in 100% equities in an attempt to gain an extra 1% return? Not so fast. We haven't evaluated the risks for each allocation strategy yet. Now that we have learned that risk and standard deviation are also part of a portfolio, we need to take a hard look at the worst possible one-year loss and standard deviations of both portfolios. The equity growth portfolio of 100% stock has a standard deviation of 17.12% and shows a worse one-year loss of 39.5% compared to the total return I portfolio of 61% equities, which shows a standard deviation of 10.54% and a worse one-year loss of only 20.80%. The question now becomes, "Is it worth trying to earn one extra percent each year while increasing your standard deviation and doubling your risk?"

I wouldn't, would you? I don't know of anyone that would almost double their downside risk for just 1% more of potential returns *if* they knew they were doing that. Many times the potential return is what is emphasized at the point of sale, not the risk. When we analyze existing portfolios and show not only the potential return but also the standard deviation and worst possible one-year loss of the portfolio, often people can't get out of them fast enough. Only your personalized Financial *Life* Plan can determine the proper asset allocation that gives you the greatest probability of success with no more risk than is necessary. When you combine your Financial *Life* Plan with an investment policy that reflects the potential spreads, you can make sure your risk tolerance matches what the plan says you need. If you do decide to chase returns, regardless of what your plan dictates, you at least know the risk of chasing that extra return so when losses occur you will be disappointed, but not surprised. Let's look at another portfolio comparison with Exhibit 9.

This is an example where we compared someone's existing portfolio with the proposed portfolio their Financial *Life* Plan recommended.

The top line of the chart reflects a portfolio of all equities, and the down periods point out the dot.com bubble burst during 2000–2002 and the 2007–2008 sub-prime loan crisis. The bottom red line reflects a portfolio with less stock, which also means a lower standard deviation and less volatility. This graph, along with the performance numbers toward the bottom of it, demonstrates the risk associated with the all-stock portfolio. I'm not saying you should not have a 100% stock-based portfolio. I am saying you need to know the downside potential of this kind of portfolio before investing in it and, at the very least, know if your Financial *Life* Plan supports doing so.

The asset allocation strategy should be built around what gives you the greatest probability of success. Just like the cookie recipe that tells you exactly how much of each ingredient should go into the batter, a Financial *Life* Plan's investment allocation

Performance Illustration

Proposed Account: IRA

Time Horizon: January 1976 – April 2016

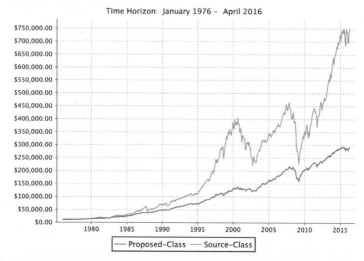

Name	Cumulative RoR	Annualized RoR	High Cycle *	Low Cycle *	+ Cycles *	- Cycles *
Proposed-Class	2,818.46%	8.72%	32.44%	- 22.87%	420	53
Source-Class	7,363.04%	11.28%	61.22%	- 43.32%	379	94

* Cycle and Cycles refer to 12 Month Periods

Exhibit 9: Performance Illustration: Volatility © SEI

strategy and recommendations should tell you exactly how much to invest in each asset class to give you the greatest probability of success with no more risk than is necessary.

Often a plan will call for a portfolio that reduces risk a lot while it may reduce the potential return a little. Exhibit 10 shows how a portfolio reduced the standard deviation.

Your plan may indicate you are better off by slightly reducing the potential rate of return from 11.28% to 8.72% (2.56%) as reflected on the vertical line, which reduced the standard deviation from 14.96% to 6.45%.

How do you know if you're being properly rewarded for the extra risk? We can use the Sharpe ratio. The Sharpe ratio is a method used to measure the risk/reward associated with an investment as it calculates its risk-adjusted return. This ratio is the industry standard for risk/reward calculations. It was developed by Nobel laureate William F. Sharpe in 1966. The Sharpe ratio is the average return earned in excess of the risk-free rate represented by US Treasury bills. If you subtract the risk-free rate from the mean return, you can identify the performance associated with risk-taking activities. Generally, the greater the value of the Sharpe ratio, the more attractive the risk-adjusted return. While overly simplistic, if you divide the historical return by the standard deviation of an investment, you will have the Sharpe ratio. By doing this with a variety of portfolios, you can determine which offers the greatest risk/reward ratio.

Modern Portfolio Theory, which is what large institutions use for their pension plans, states that adding assets to a diversified portfolio that have correlations of less than one with each other can decrease portfolio risk without sacrificing return. Such diversification will serve to increase the Sharpe ratio of a portfolio. For you mathematicians, the Sharpe ratio = (mean portfolio return – risk-free rate)/standard deviation of portfolio return. [12]

The Sharpe ratio basically lets you know if you are being

---

12 Investopedia, "Sharpe Ratio," 2016, http://www.investopedia.com/terms/s/sharperatio.asp.

Risk vs. Return

Proposed Account: IRA

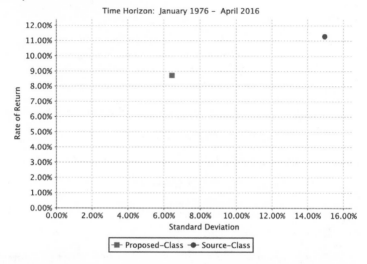

Time Horizon: January 1976 – April 2016

Name	Rate of Return	Standard Deviation	Sharpe Ratio
Proposed-Class	8.72%	6.45%	1.33
Source-Class	11.28%	14.96%	0.74

Exhibit 10: Reduction of Risk vs. Return © SEI

properly rewarded for the extra risk you are taking in a portfolio. This is helpful when you are trying to compare your portfolio that has a higher potential rate of return and a higher standard deviation to a portfolio our sophisticated Financial *Life* Planning software has created that says you have a greater probability of success with containing a lower rate of return and a lower standard deviation. In simple terms, you divide the projected rate of return by the standard deviation, and presto, you have the Sharpe ratio. The higher the Sharpe ratio, the better.

Let's go back to Exhibit 10. As you can see, the recommended portfolio increased the Sharpe ratio from .74 to 1.33—almost double!

When I was completing my masters in financial planning, I had to take an existing portfolio and increase its Sharpe ratio by determining the potential returns and standard deviations to two levels (remember two standard deviations means there's a 95% chance the spread of the returns will fall in between the low and high). We were not allowed to use a computer or any software; it had to all be done by hand. It took me over 6 hours to increase the Sharpe ratio on the case study portfolio, which was extremely frustrating because my financial planning software does it in one second!

> The higher the Sharpe ratio, the better.

In the last chapter, we talked about asset allocation, how it accounts for 91.25% of a portfolio's return, and how it has to be the foundation of how you invest, instead of chasing funds that did well the previous year. In this chapter, we learned the importance of looking at a portfolio's volatility, or standard deviation, instead of only considering potential returns. The Sharpe ratio is a helpful calculation that compares the potential rate of return and the standard deviation to determine the best portfolio. Remember, the higher the Sharpe ratio, the better.

You now know to avoid a portfolio that offers a greater potential return of 1% that almost doubles the risk. Furthermore, with the help of our friend William Sharpe and the Sharpe ratio, you learned that you could compare the returns and standard deviations of two different portfolios and see which has the better risk and reward. It's important to understand these concepts before the next chapter, because the software that generates recommended portfolios uses projected returns and standard deviations as a big part of what's going on under your financial hood.

Now that we have the basics, we can move on, put these lessons to work, and create a Financial *Life* Plan—the foundation for your future investment decisions.

CHAPTER 7

TAKING THE WHEEL:

HOW TO CREATE A SOUND

FINANCIAL PLAN

YOU PROBABLY FEEL LIKE you've just had someone tell you several routes that you can take toward your destination and warned you of the dangers of taking the wrong route. How do you now bring this information together to make sure you're driving in the right direction? Now is the time to put the cell phone down, stop texting, and pay attention, because we are about to get into where the rubber meets the road.

I want to use an actual Financial *Life* Plan to show you how this can all play out for you in Exhibit 11. For the sake of example, let's say you have several goals in your plan, such as an annual vacation, weddings for your daughters, and college education expenses for your daughters and your son. Additionally, you want to retire at age 62 with an income of $10,000 per month, factoring an increase in your income of 3% each year for inflation. Your current strategy is almost all stock, because your 401(k) is invested in all equity mutual funds. You thought that such a strategy would give you a better chance of making some great returns before heading into retirement. Exhibit 11 has a lot going on, and there's even more under the hood, but once understood, it's very powerful. Your Financial *Life* Plan shows your results based on your goals and how you are currently invested. If you receive average returns each year with zero volatility or risk associated with your current portfolio, you will accomplish 64% of your goals, or 64% of your wedding and college goals as well as $6,400 per month in retirement. We also want to show you what your odds are if you suffered two bad years in the stock market right after you retired; something similar to what happened to those who retired in 2006. In this case, you would only be able to accomplish 58% of your goal, or $5,800 per month, a far cry from $10,000. As we all know, the stock market does not produce expected average returns every year. Instead, there is volatility or standard deviations from the expected return. There is volatility every day the stock market is open. Perhaps over several decades the portfolio will come close to the amounts reflected in the average return column, but that doesn't help you today. Because we cannot predict the future, the only option is to run a market stress test. This is where I need to introduce you to Monte Carlo.

I'm not talking about an exotic place in Europe; I'm talking about a Monte Carlo stress test on a portfolio. The Monte Carlo

Probability of Success indicates the likelihood of funding all of your goals based on your portfolio's volatility. For instance, a 64% Probability of Success suggests that if your plan were run 10,000 times with a different sequence of returns each time based on its current allocation, you would fund 100% of your goals 6,400 times, and the remaining 3,600 times you would have a shortfall in funding one or more of your goals. In short, this would mean you had a 64% probability of success. However, in this particular situation, and as Exhibit 11 indicates, the Monte Carlo stress test showed you had just a 41% probability of success. Ouch!

This is obviously not acceptable, but how great is it that you know you are off course with plenty of time to correct your steering!

Now let's take a look at what our Financial *Life* Planning software indicated you needed to do to increase your odds of keeping your financial tank full, taking care of the wedding and college expenses for your kids and having a successful retirement for yourselves.

The changes, as shown in the plan results in the following recommended scenario, resulted in you being able to meet 100% of all your goals in the event you earned average returns or even if you experienced bad timing in the first two years after you retired. More importantly, your probability of success went up to 99%, the highest a Monte Carlo simulation test goes. To accomplish this, the plan indicated you needed to do the following:

Results – Current and Recommended

Results	Current Scenario	Recommended Scenario	
	Average Return 85% — Bad Timing 74%	Average Return 100% — Bad Timing 100%	
Estimated % of Goals Funded	Probability of Success	Probability of Success	
Likelihood of Funding All Goals	**41%** Below Confidence Zone	**99%** Above Confidence Zone	

Your Confidence Zone: 70% - 90%

Retirement	Current Scenario	Recommended Scenario	Changes In Value
Retirement Age			
John	62 in 2029	65 in 2032	3 year(s) later
Mary	61 in 2029	64 in 2032	3 year(s) later
Planning Age			
John	90 in 2057	90 in 2057	
Mary	92 in 2060	92 in 2060	
Goals			
Needs			
Retirement - Living Expense			
Both Retired	$63,000	$60,000	Decreased $3,000
Mary Alone Retired	$52,000	$52,000	
Total Spending for Life of Plan	**$1,983,000**	**$1,716,000**	**Decreased 13%**

Exhibit 11: Current vs Recommended Scenarios/Accomplishing Goals ©PIEtech, Inc.

1. You needed to retire at age sixty-five instead of sixty-two to fund the vacations, weddings, and college costs. We have found that most people don't mind working a little longer, as long as they know it's necessary to give them the probability of success they desire. Another option is to retire at age sixty-two, but supplement the first few years with consulting or part-time income

2. You needed to decrease your spending by 13% between your retirement age of sixty-five and the end of your life. After the first few years of your retirement, after taking the cruise, remodeling your kitchen, and going to Hawaii (this must be a mandate as everyone seems to do it), you need to reduce your spending, something most people do anyway. Our firm has helped countless people with their Financial *Life* Plans, and approximately 25% are currently retired. Before retirement, when we tell them they will probably decrease their spending after the first few years of retirement, they never believe me. However, in thirty years, I have never had a retiree not reduce their spending. It normally happens during an annual review a few years after retirement when they say, "You know, David, we are just not spending the amount of money we are withdrawing, so let's reduce the withdrawals."

My son JD sat in on one of my appointments last summer. When I was telling a new client that people always seem to reduce their monthly spending a few years into retirement, the client asked me why. When I said, "Unlike when I first started Financial *Life* Planning, we didn't have the Internet then."

I thought JD was going to fall out of his chair laughing. My son, as a twenty-two-year-old doesn't know that the Internet has not always been around. The Internet allows retirees to compare prices for everything, and search engines can help people find the lowest prices on flights, cruises, and hotels. Vendors know this, so they stay as competitive as possible. Additionally, during the pre-Internet days, travel agents had big offices with lots of agents and received a 10% commission on most of their bookings. Not anymore! Last, when you are surfing the Internet looking at travel prices, you can see that the prices are reduced during certain days of the week or months of the year. Once you are retired, you can travel during off days or off-season and reduce your costs substantially. The result is that it doesn't cost as much to do many of the things retirees like to do.

3. You needed to increase your savings by $20,000 per year between now and retirement. This can be accomplished with your future 401(k) contributions and company match once you return to work. Because the money going into your 401(k) is before taxes, you will save income taxes, so the net effect on cash flow will be less.

4. You needed to reduce your stock in your investments by a significant percentage. As you have already learned, although this means you will possibly reduce potential returns slightly. It means you will decrease your standard deviation or risk also.

Let's pull over to the side of the road for a minute and reflect on what this one page of the Financial *Life* Plan can do for you, because it can literally be life changing. This one page can show you, based on how you're currently invested, what your probability of success is, along with the steps you can take to increase it to the level you need for your personal comfort. Once you complete your Financial *Life* Plan, you should revisit it every year (or sooner if something substantial happens in your life), with your Financial *Life* Planner to make small adjustments along your journey, so you can stay on track.

How great would it be to know exactly what you needed to do, step-by-step, to give you the greatest probability of achieving financial success? No more guessing on how much you should save or how you should allocate your 401(k). You'll know exactly what you need to do to give you the greatest probability of success in accomplishing your life goals. This is empowering!

> You'll know exactly what you need to do to give you the greatest probability of success in accomplishing your life goals. This is empowering!

One question we often get is, "So is there only one allocation that will get me to where I want to go?" The answer is no. You can see how this works in Exhibit 12.

The portfolios are listed on the left. They range from the least amount of stock (capital appreciation I at the top) to the greatest amount of stock at the bottom (equity growth). Once you complete a risk tolerance questionnaire, the specific portfolio can be chosen. Before moving on, I want to brake long enough to make two points.

First, all of the elements we saw in Exhibit 11—financial goals, financial amounts, annual savings, desired probability of success and asset allocation—are all interactive. By that, I mean we will ask you for—

- A timeline of when you want or need to fund your financial goals

- The dollar amount associated with each of your financial goals

- Your annual savings amount

- Your desired probability of success

- Your asset allocation preferences, if any

Then, we will generate your Financial *Life* Plan based on your answers. These different aspects are interactive; they affect each other. If you tell us to "lock in" a certain age for a specific goal and won't accept anything other than a 99% probability of success, then that restriction will put more strain on the other aspects of your goals, such as how much you need to be saving annually. Normally it is better to provide ideal and acceptable answers and only lock in a topic that you feel very strongly about.

Second, as I just described, the Financial *Life* Plan is not a "plan in a can," or a rigid, premade plan. Most financial coaches do not do lifelong plans. The software is expensive and the plans are time consuming, so they'd rather just discuss investments. If they do a plan, it's a quick and easy one using averages or assumptions. As an example, for retirement, it might automatically set it at age 65 and use 75% of your current income. Your goals are too important to use a plan in a can.

OK, are you ready to see an example of what a well-diversified portfolio looks like?

Once your personal Financial *Life* Plan points to the allocation that gives you the greatest probability of success

> Your goals are too important to use a plan in a can.

with no more risk than necessary, your financial coach will show you what that looks like. Following are two examples of the same allocation your plan indicated you could have.

The moderate portfolio has a few manager mandates that are worthy of recognition, the Global Managed Volatility fund and the US Managed Volatility fund. As the names imply, these are money managers that attempt to buy securities they feel will

Worksheet Detail - Portfolio Probability Matrix

Portfolio Probability Matrix for What If Scenario 1

Risk Based Portfolio	Portfolio used in What If Scenario 1	Results		Bear Market Loss	
	Both before and during Retirement with same portfolio	Probability of Success	Safety Margin (Current Dollars)	Great Recession Return	Bond Bear Market Return
Capital Preservation I		99%	$392,964	-4%	-2%
Capital Preservation II		96%	$480,490	-10%	1%
Balanced I		93%	$545,936	-15%	2%
Balanced II		90%	$633,390	-21%	4%
Total Return I		88%	$716,556	-26%	6%
Total Return II		84%	$853,751	-33%	9%
Capital Growth I		82%	$1,045,446	-39%	11%
Current		79%	$1,179,960	-45%	12%
Capital Growth II		79%	$1,179,960	-45%	12%
Equity Growth		77%	$1,327,169	-51%	15%

Probability of Success

Legend: Balanced II ★ Risk-Based Portfolio(Balanced II) ▲ Current Portfolio ■ Confidence Zone

Exhibit 12: Portfolio Probability Matrix: Picking the allocation that works best. ©PIEtech, Inc.

Prepared by: David Blaydes

do well during volatile times. Now that you are an expert on standard deviation and Sharpe ratios, I can tell you that managed volatility managers buy high Sharpe Ratio securities. Since it is not possible to obtain managed volatility managers with index or exchange-traded funds (ETF) funds, the portfolio uses money managers, so the internal fees are more than index or ETF or funds. However, these funds use only institutionally priced portfolios, so the expenses are reasonable.

For more growth-oriented portfolios that do not need managed volatility managers, or for investors that are very fee sensitive, the allocation the plan indicates will give you the highest probability of success that can be structured using index or ETFs as shown in Exhibit 13.

SIMILAR TO HOW A mutual fund works, an exchange-traded fund (ETF) pools the money of many investors, like yourself, and purchases a group of securities. Similar to index mutual funds, most ETFs are passively managed instead of actively managed. This means instead of having a fund manager to buy and sell stocks and bonds, ETFs try to achieve the investment returns of a specific index associated with the ETF. Since the ETF tracks its index, a money manager and team of analysts are not involved, which therefore substantially reduces the management fees, or expense ratio, of an ETF, thus the basis for their popularity.

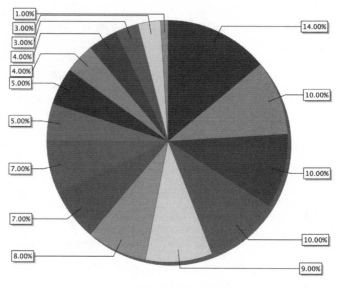

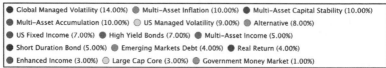

Exhibit 13: Asset Class Allocation: Sample Portfolio Using Money Managers © SEI

Let's take a look at a tactically managed ETF portfolio that closely matches the allocation found in Exhibit 14. By *tactical*, I mean that the economists with the firm that produced this graph, SEI, attempt to determine if our economy is in a period of stress, distress, recovery or expansion, and if it is overweight/ underweight and place in the asset classes accordingly.

Notice anything different between this ETF portfolio and the one I showed you prior? You should see two things that are different:

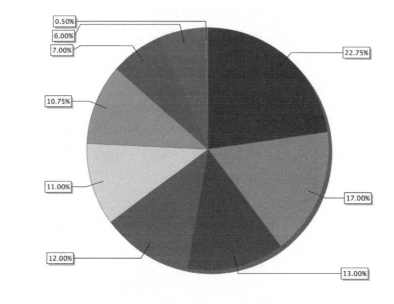

Exhibit 14: Asset Class Allocation: Sample Portfolio Using ETFs © SEI

1. **There are fewer funds.** Although there are many ETF funds available in the marketplace, you will not find ETFs for every asset class, unlike a portfolio constructed using more traditional money manager-based funds.

2. **There aren't any managed volatility funds.** This is because they require a manager to make decisions about what equities to purchase for a portfolio that is expected to do well during volatile times in the stock market.

Now that you know the importance of tying asset allocation to your personal goals, so that you have the highest probability of success with no more risk than is necessary, are you ready to dig a little deeper and see how to build your portfolio using a well-established and highly disciplined approach? Exhibit 15 represents the investment process we have found to work the best.

This should be the chapter where you are now saying, "I get it." Instead of going to a broker with your 401(k) and investing in what their firm wants them to push or what was hot last year, you now—

- Have a Financial *Life* Plan that includes all of your financial goals and assets

- Know that asset allocation accounts for 91.5% of investment returns and paying attention to the allocation your plan says gives you the greatest probability of success based on a Monte Carlo simulation of 10,000 stock market return sequences

- Can invest in that allocation either in a portfolio of money managers or lower cost ETFs

- Can rerun your plan annually and tweak the allocations, so that you always stay on the right road on your life journey towards financial independence

Now let me ask you this: Which of the following two people do you think has the best odds for financial independence? The person who just wings it, saving whatever they feel comfortable with

Investment Process › Summary

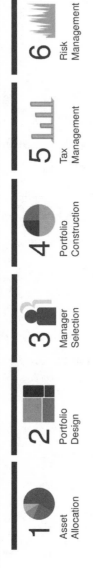

1 Asset Allocation

2 Portfolio Design

3 Manager Selection

4 Portfolio Construction

5 Tax Management

6 Risk Management

- Asset allocation that is customized to your situation

- Access to top quality managers with some of the best ideas from around the globe

- Personalized investment strategies driven by client goals

- Diversification at multiple levels

- Ongoing risk management and oversight

- Advisor independence and process transparency

SEI New ways.
New answers.®

Exhibit 15: Our Approach to Portfolio Design© SEI

25

and making investment allocations according to their "gut" feeling, previous performance, or the opinion of a friend? Or, the person who does a Financial *Life* Plan, saves and invests according to what the plan says will give them the highest probability of success with no more risk than is necessary, and periodically reviews the plan and asset allocation between now and retirement?

Which person do you want to be? You have learned about financial software that will show you what your current probability of success is, based on your investments, savings rate, future spending, and your life goals. More importantly, your Financial *Life* Plan will show you what you need to do to increase your probability of success to the percentage that matches your comfort level. You will no longer be making decisions by hunches or emotions. You'll know exactly what you need to do to get to where you want to be. In other words, you can start making your financial decisions based on design instead of default.

> You can start making your financial decisions based on design instead of default.

CHAPTER 8

REACHING THE END

OF THE ROAD: CONVERTING

INVESTMENTS TO INCOME

THE DISCUSSIONS CONCERNING PORTFOLIOS so far have been on long-term investment portfolios, such as your 401(k),

that are to be used at a later date. Well, what if you need income from one of your investments now? Does that change things? Although the content of this chapter pertains to anyone who needs income from any kind of account, I'll use retirement as my example.

Asset allocation works over time, but not every time. From its peak in September of 2008 to its low in March of 2009, the Dow Jones Industrial Average (DJIA) lost over 50% of its value. If your 401(k) or other investments had substantial equities in them, by the time you received your first-quarter 2009 investment statement, you could have lost half of your money. The S&P, a broader-based index of the top 500 securities, had a loss of 38.5% in 2008.

Now let me add a twist to this. What if you had retired toward the end of 2007 and had elected to withdraw 5% of your investments for income? Let's do the math here. If your portfolio decreased in value by 54% and you were withdrawing 5%, then you are down 59%! Imagine this happening after you retired. Instead of playing golf and spending time with your grandchildren, you'd be looking for another job!

Having an all-equity 401(k) left many newly retired people unable to do several of the things they had planned on doing in retirement, and some even end up going back to work. Do you think it's possible that the market could decline the first year or two after you decide to retire or start supplementing your salary with income from your investments? Sure it could! You need to invest in a well-diversified portfolio and hold, hope, and pray, or utilize a strategy designed from the chassis up to help handle situations like this. That's our preference, and it's known as a *distribution-focused strategy* (DFS), or a strategy that focuses on making sure your distributions last as long as you do. This DFS can get a little involved, so let's look at the basics first.

CREATED WITH YOU IN MIND

DFS was designed to address the growing need for a savings plan that lasts a lifetime. It offers greater control, flexibility, and lower fees than many other investment alternatives by bringing you its own distinct risk versus return objective. The strategy you select is based on your desired cash flow, risk tolerance, tax situation, and the amount of time. By allocating your assets among these three different pools, a DFS is better able to provide you with a steady stream of cash flow and preserve your principal investment for as long as possible.

DFS can help in many areas. Some of these include—

- Strategies to address your need for predictable cash flow

- An approach to help you make your assets last a lifetime

- Access to your money any time, without a penalty

Customized to Your Personal Financial Needs

Because everyone's financial situation is different, DFS portfolios are tailored to your unique cash flow needs, tax situation, and risk tolerance. To achieve this highly customized strategy, your DFS assets are spread among three pools within a selected strategy—each with its own distinct risk/return objective. Some of the DFS benefits include—

- Low cost compared with other investments

- Tax management from non-retirement accounts to help reduce your taxes and enhance income

- The ability to pass remaining assets onto your heirs

Created with you in mind

The Distribution-Focused Strategies were designed to address the growing need for a savings plan that lasts a lifetime. DFS offers greater control, flexibility and lower fees than many other investment alternatives by bringing you:

> Strategies created to address your need for predictable cash flows in retirement

> An approach aimed at helping you make your assets last a lifetime

> Access to your money any time, **without a surrender penalty**

> Low costs compared with other investments

> Tax management to help reduce your taxes and enhance your income

> The ability to pass remaining assets on to your heirs

Customized to your personal financial needs

Because everyone's situation is different, DFS portfolios are tailored to your individual cash flow needs, tax situation and risk tolerance. To achieve this highly customized experience, your DFS assets are spread among three pools within a selected strategy—each with its own distinct risk/return objective. The strategy you select is based on your desired cash flow and time horizon. By allocating your assets among these three different pools, DFS is better able to pursue the goals of providing you with a steady stream of fixed-dollar cash flows and preserving your principal investment for as long as possible.

Fig. 2: Helping clients manage income with Distribution-Focused Strategies

Pool 1	Pool 2	Pool 3
Short-term (0-7 years)	**Intermediate-term** (8-14 years)	**Long-term** (15+ years)
Supports investment goals that seek to manage risk of loss.	Supports investment goals that seek growth while managing the risk of loss.	Supports investment goals that seek maximum growth over long-term horizons.

Below is an example of how the three Pools are allocated within the Stability Tilt DFS Strategy.

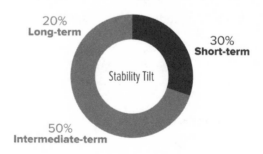

20%
Long-term

30%
Short-term

Stability Tilt

50%
Intermediate-term

Exhibit 16: Three-Pool Approach to a Diversification-Focused Strategy © SEI

Your financial needs and risk tolerance will determine how aggressive you will want your DFS to be. We typically classify these as stability, growth, or some in between—stability and growth. Let's use an example of a stability DFS. Exhibit 16 shows your investments would be segregated into three separate investment allocations, Pool 1 for your shorter-term needs, Pool 2 for your intermediate-term needs, and Pool 3 for your longer-term needs. The longer the need, the more aggressive the allocation for that pool can be, because you'll have more time to weather market volatility. On the other hand, you want to have Pool 1 invested conservatively, as this is the pool you are withdrawing funds from first.

Smart Distribution

The way your distributions are sourced can have a big impact on your portfolio's performance over time. With DFS, distributions are first funded with the income generated by your investments—primarily dividends, interest payments, and capital gains distributions. If your income is not enough to meet your target, a portion of your principal will be sold to achieve that goal.

When principal is sold, the first assets targeted are those with over-weighted positions. This includes assets that have appreciated in price to the point where they now represent a larger-than-desired percentage of your portfolio. This way, you avoid selling assets that are under stress and instead focus on selling assets that have met or exceeded their price targets.

Smart distributions

The way your distributions are sourced can have a big impact on your performance over time. With DFS, distributions are first funded with the income generated by your investments—primarily dividends, interest payments and capital gains distributions. If the income is not enough to meet your target, a portion of your principal will be sold in order to achieve that goal.

When principal is sold, the first assets targeted are those with overweighted positions. This would include assets that have appreciated in price to the point where they now represent a larger-than-desired percentage of your portfolio. In this way, you avoid selling assets that are under stress, instead focusing on selling assets that have met or exceeded their price targets.

For greater tax efficiency, assets with capital losses would also be targeted when principal is needed to fund your distributions. Investments with embedded long-term capital gains would be sold only as a last resort, as would assets in underweighted parts of your portfolio.

Smart distributions make the most of your DFS investment

Fig. 3: Distribution source order

Keeping your options open

Knowing that the future can hold unexpected changes, we've designed your DFS portfolio for maximum flexibility. With DFS, your money remains yours. You keep full control of your assets at all times. You can increase, reduce or stop your distributions as your needs change, and are free to redeem your shares without penalty at any time. Growth is also an objective, so when the time comes, any remaining assets can be passed on to your heirs, allowing you to leave a legacy to the people and organizations you care most about.

Backed by an industry leader

Founded in 1968, SEI manages more than $239 billion in total assets, and has relationships with 108 banks and trust institutions in the U.S., including the trust departments of nine of the 20 largest U.S. banks.[1] Our products and services help corporations, institutions and individuals like you create and manage wealth in a way that supports your personal goals. For more than 40 years, we have used leading-edge research to anticipate changing investor needs and create innovative solutions designed for individual and institutional investors alike.

Exhibit 17: Distribution Flow for Distribution-Focused Strategy © SEI

For greater tax efficiency of non-retirement funds, assets with capital losses would also be targeted when principal is needed to fund your distributions. Investments with embedded long-term capital gains would be sold only as a last resort, as would assets in underweighted parts of your portfolio. Remember, the aggressive portfolio is for long-term funds, the moderate portfolio is for intermediate-term needs, and the defensive portfolio is for your short-term needs. Short-term is defensive so that you reduce the chances of taking a substantial stock market hit on your portfolio at a time when you are also taking withdrawals. The advantage to this is that when that stock market does suffer a correction, the more aggressive portfolio represents a future need. The portfolio you are taking current withdrawals from is invested defensively, as shown in Exhibit 17.

Making the Most of Your DFS Investment

Knowing that the future can hold unexpected changes, we design DFS portfolios for maximum flexibility. With DFS, your money remains yours. You keep full control of your assets at all times. You can increase, decrease, or stop your distributions as your needs change and are free to completely liquidate your investment without penalty at any time. Growth is also an objective of DFS, so when the time comes, any remaining assets can be passed on to your heirs, allowing you to leave a legacy to the people and organizations you care most about.

The bottom line is that while I am a believer in hope and prayer, I also believe it is prudent to incorporate the best strategy possible to make sure your income lasts as long as you do!

The Great Recession of 2007 taught us a lot. In particular, it taught us not to invest with an allocation that's more aggressive than what you need to accomplish your Financial *Life* Plan. If you are taking distributions from assets at the same time they are decreasing in value, you could end up going back to work. Once distributions begin, you need a strategy designed to protect the longevity of your distributions, which is exactly what DFS does.

This chapter could be a lifesaver for you. At some point, you are going to start taking withdrawals from your investments. If you do that at the same time you are not working and the stock market corrects, you could find yourself canceling your travel plans and going back to work. A DFS that is designed to make your distributions last as long as possible is important, and now you know it exists!

CHAPTER 9

GETTING A GOOD MECHANIC: TIPS FOR FINDING THE BEST FINANCIAL COACH

ON JUNE 21, 2016, I typed *financial planning* into the Amazon search box and got 45,662 results. When I typed in *financial planning during a job transition*, I got zero results. Because I was motivated to write this book as a way to educate and to help you with your financial planning needs during your job transition, I want to talk about what you should look for in a financial coach, so you can make the best decision for you, whether you go with RPI or another firm.

Fortune 500 companies and outplacement firms across the US have used RPI for over two decades to assist their employees and candidates for several reasons. I'm going to share the reasons here, so that you can see what they look for in a financial coaching firm. You should be as picky with whom you use for your financial coaching as companies are with whom they allow to help their valued employees with the same type of coaching.

Things to consider include—

- Designations

- Experience

- Independence

- Specialty

- Comfort

Designations

Designations are important for a variety of reasons. First, to obtain many of them, you must spend a considerable amount of time becoming educated on the various elements of financial and investment planning. Second, it helps you rule out those who say they do financial planning but are actually just a broker selling an investment or an insurance agent selling insurance. Let's take a look at some of the better-known designations, as you will want your financial coach to have some meaningful initials after their name.

When you are considering what to look for in a financial planner, Certified Financial Planner, CFP®, is probably the most well-known designation. The current requirements include successful completion of courses on the subjects of financial planning, insurance, investments, taxes, and estate planning followed by a comprehensive exam. For many people, it takes two to three years to complete the CFP® designation. To maintain the CFP®, you must have thirty hours of qualifying continuing education credit every two years.

Bachelor's Degree in Financial Planning

Financial planning is now an undergraduate major with many universities. My son JD graduated from Purdue University in 2016 with a major in financial planning. Not only does the curriculum offer textbook knowledge in a variety of business subjects, it also provides practical knowledge, because some of the professionals on staff are practicing financial planners.

Master's Degree in Financial Planning

You can also now obtain a master's in financial planning. The study is very similar to that of a CFP®, with each subject going substantially deeper in complexity. Once the CFP® is completed, you have your choice of master-level courses on financial, tax, investment, insurance, and estate planning. These courses encompass approximately 1,000 hours over a two-year period. I have discovered pursuing industry specific degrees not only results in greater knowledge, it can also generate noneducational benefits that can help an advisor serve his clients. As an example, I met fellow advisor Andrew Palomo in my master's class, and the professional and personal friendship from that alone justified the time and effort in obtaining my degree.

MBA

A master's of business administration is a graduate degree achieved at a university that provides theoretical and practical training to help gain a better understanding of several subjects that are ideal for financial planning, such as finance and accounting. An MBA is ideal for a firm that prepares financial plans due to the overlap of subject matter between the degree and the Financial *Life* Plan.

AIF®

This designation stands for Accredited Investment Fiduciary, and it is obtained by meeting the qualifications of the AIF® Board and the successful completion of their exam. The basis of this designation is found in the word *fiduciary*, as it mandates the financial planner to be solely in the client's best interest. I have found that the advisors who believe to their core that anything they recommend is in the best interest of the person they are trying to help are the ones that take the time and effort to become an AIF®. In fact, it was Josh Kadish, a fellow advisor I have had the pleasure of knowing and working with for over two decades, who obtained his AIF® first. Knowing Josh always does only what is in his client's best interest and the extreme high level of integrity that he, and for that matter his attorney father, Steve, live by both personally and professionally, I also did the study and exam necessary to obtain the designation.

RFC®

This designation stands for Registered Financial Consultant. The requirements for this designation are a little different from the others. In addition to being properly licensed, you need proof of a college degree and that you have been actively engaged in financial planning for at least three years and are free of any regulatory issues. The other designations do not require the degree and experience, which is why I became an RFC®.

Experience

When I started Financial *Life* Planning in my early twenties and was working with people in their sixties, I used to wish for a little gray hair. (I should have been more careful in what I wished for.) When you are looking for someone to assist you with something as important as achieving financial independence for the rest of your life, make sure you get someone who has been associated with a team who has many years of experience.

The mistakes that I made in the early years of my career are the reason I only go to doctors who have been practicing for many years. I went into financial planning right out of college. I was highly motivated, working hundred-hour weeks. Before making any investment recommendation, I spent hours drafting a comprehensive Financial *Life* Plan. (We didn't have personal computers, financial planning software, or the Internet.) Although I have gone through many batteries, I still have my original HP 12-C calculator. Even though I have always been driven to make recommendations that I felt in my heart were only in the best interests of my clients, my inexperience in the beginning led to mistakes. That's painful to admit, because I know those mistakes resulted in people losing money in investments. I had a good heart and integrity; I just didn't have the experience. When making the decision about whom you work with for financial advice, try to work with someone who has been around long enough to have made some mistakes and learned from them, so they can better serve you.

> You want your financial coach to be working for you, not an investment firm.

Independence

You want your financial coach to be working for you, not an investment firm.

Right out of college, I didn't have a lot of financial technical knowledge, but I did have a lot of college debt. That combination resulted in me working with the financial planning department of a large insurance company. They gave me a salary, benefits, and training. In return, when I made an investment recommendation, guess which company's product I had to recommend? Yep, the company whose name appeared on my paycheck.

After a couple of years, out of a desire to recommend only the best of the best to my clients, I went out on my own. That independence has allowed me to recommend only the best financial solutions for those we have the pleasure of providing Financial *Life* Plans for. I have to pay my own phone bill, but I wouldn't trade my independence for anything. No one tells me what to recommend to a client, and I don't have any conflicts of interest. I suggest whoever you decide to work with be independent, so that they, too, can recommend the best of the best without any conflicts of interest.

Specialty

You want your financial coach to specialize in whatever it is that you are hiring them for. I tore the ACL in my knee many years ago. One of the first things I did was to research experienced orthopedic surgeons who specialized in knees. I did not research general practitioners or internists, as I wanted someone who specialized in not only orthopedics but also my problem area—knees.

In the same way, financial advisors are typically generalists. They work with those just starting their careers as well as those retiring, including physicians, business owners, and anyone else with money to invest. I remember when I first started, a prospect had to have two things for me to work with them: a heartbeat and a check that cleared the bank!

Whatever your specific area of need, try to find a financial coach with some designation and experience who specializes in your area of need. We work in a complex world. It would be very difficult to stay on top of investments and ever-changing tax laws. Additionally, the more areas a planner must spread their client base over, the less they get to know any of them well. For over two decades, we have worked only with those people in transition, 90% of which are in transition between jobs and 10% are transitioning into retirement. This has afforded us the opportunity to know the investments, tax laws, and more importantly, the emotional state of people going through a transition, so that we can help them as much as possible. As you search for an advisor, try to find someone who, in addition to designations, experience, and independence, has worked with several others in your situation.

Comprehensive and Holistic

The restraints of desired book length did not allow me to go into other areas that your plan should cover. However, it's critical that you work with an adviser that will incorporate all related planning issues as part of your Financial *Life* Plan. Taking a comprehensive and holistic approach to your planning will make sure nothing gets overlooked.

Comfort

Bedside manner counts. Many years ago, my mother had a suspicious lump. Her doctor referred her to a physician that specialized in such lumps. He warned us that while the physician was a great surgeon, his bedside manner was not very good. He quickly added, "However, that shouldn't matter, because you are going to him for his medical expertise."

Should it matter that the doctor we were referred to was not very nice? My mother's biopsy showed the lump was not cancer, but she was encouraged to return semiannually for checkups. Because of how unfriendly he was, my mother refused to ever go back to him. So, yes, it mattered.

In the same way, your financial coach, especially if they do a comprehensive plan for you (and I would hope at this point you won't consider them if they don't), is going to help you accomplish your goals, such as helping with your children's college education, paying for weddings and trips, and funding your future retirement. Additionally, the plan will need to be updated on an annual basis. If you don't like your financial coach and end up not going back for your reviews, you will be the one to suffer. Therefore, if you don't like the person you are thinking about using, move on until you find one that you do like. I tell those I work with, "You are my client, not your money."

> Do not ever invest your funds with a financial advisor in a manner where the advisor can get their hands on your money.

My clients are not just an account! That's the type of relationship you want to find.

Due Diligence

You have to do your research and read up on your potential financial coach. You cannot be too careful, as we are talking about your hard-earned money. The first thing I want to say here is this: Do not ever invest your funds with a financial advisor in a manner where the advisor can get their hands on your money. You don't want to give them an opportunity to steal it.

Additionally, you need to do a little homework on anyone you are thinking about working with. The good news is that it's relatively easy. The "watchdogs" of our industry are the Financial Industry Regulatory Authority, or FINRA. They oversee people and firms that sell stocks, bonds, mutual funds, and other securities. You can go to their website, www.finra.org, and in the top right corner, in large print, you'll see, "Broker Check." Try it out, type in David L. Blaydes (David Lee Blaydes, zip code 60563. If there's any doubt, my CRD number is 850725) and hit submit. You'll see the number of years I've been in the industry, my licenses, and most importantly, under "Disclosure," you will be able to see if I have any customer complaints or arbitrations, regulatory actions, employment terminations, bankruptcy filings, and civil or criminal proceedings that I was a part of. This research takes all of about one minute, so there's no excuse for you not to do this for anyone you are either currently working with or considering working with in the financial services industry.

As I've said, I wrote this book primarily to educate people, not to solicit business. I wanted to give you the information, so that you can find your own financial coach completely independent of me or my firm. However, be careful, as anyone can put "financial planner" on their business card. You read that right. There are no restrictions on who can call themselves a financial planner. I wish that were not the case, but it is. A person calling themself a financial planner could be an insurance agent or a broker trying to sell financial products or a financial planner offering comprehensive financial plans. How do you know the difference? First, did they take the time to ask you in-depth questions concerning your short-term and long-term goals? Second, did they present you with a comprehensive Financial *Life* Plan or just show you some insurance or investments? Third, do they have any designations behind their name? Having one or all of the designations we discussed does not necessarily mean they are a great financial advisor. However, I have found that most individuals who take the time and effort to pass the necessary exams to obtain some designations typically do so because they believe in comprehensive financial planning, similar to our Financial *Life* Plan.

As shown in Exhibit 18, the road to financial success requires reading signs and following directions. No one arrives at the destination of financial success by chance.

Road to Financial Success

The road to financial success requires reading signs and following directions. No one arrives at the destination of financial success by chance.

Most people fail to implement a solid strategy, only to realize too late the short distance they traveled and how little they have accomplished! Begin your journey now by setting goals and establishing priorities. Commit to a plan of action!

Start today on your road to financial success!

Exhibit 18: The Road to Financial Success ©Advicent Solutions, LP

Most people fail to implement a solid strategy, only to real-ize too late the short distance they traveled and how little they have accomplished! Begin your journey now by setting goals and establishing priorities. Commit to a plan of action!

Start today on your road to financial success!

I know we've covered a lot of material in this book. I've intentionally tried to stay away from using too much financial lingo, because my goal was for you to understand every word. However, I know you are probably still overwhelmed, because in addition to handling the financial issues related to your job transition, you have probably also been actively involved in your job search. So what's the next step?

RPI

If you have your own financial coach, great. If you want to try to do this on your own, great. If you want to contact RPI for help, that's great as well. The primary goal of this book is to educate and motivate you to complete a Financial *Life* Plan. As far as we are concerned, if you want to consider RPI, please know I use the education achieved in obtaining all of the designations listed in the previous chapter, along with my experience, independence, transition specialty, and a reassuring approach to properly guide RPI's financial coaches. We are independent, are free of any investment conflicts of interest, have over two decades of experience specializing in working with individuals such as yourself, have a spotless track record, and will always make an investment recommendation with full disclosure and complete transparency based on what your Financial *Life* Plan says provides the highest probability of success with no more risk than necessary.

Before you go any further, you should know that RPI analyzes current investment holdings to generate a probability of success for your current scenario. In order to do this, our software needs assets to analyze. Therefore, Financial *Life* Plans can only be generated for those with a  minimum of $50,000 to invest. If you do not meet the total investment minimum, you are still welcome to use the over 200 articles, PowerPoint presentations, videos, and calculators in our financial resource center at www.rpiplan.com.

If you meet the $50,000 minimum:

1. Go to www.rpiplan.com and in the financial resource center select "Click Here to Get Started." Complete and submit an online confidential financial profile. Once you submit the form electronically, we will be notified and will contact you. If you have any questions before, or when, completing the form, simply contact us via the contact information on our website.

2. Once we receive your form, we will schedule an appointment with you to review your data and goals with one of our financial coaches. We utilize web conferencing for our meetings, and we will email you a link that you'll simply click on to start a meeting. You'll see on your computer screen the same thing we see on ours, making it very easy to have a lifelike meeting. We will also have a webcam on and encourage you to do the same. No matter where you are, we'll be able to have a face-to-face meeting. We've come a long way since that HP 12-C calculator!

3. If you use the password *book*, there will not be any charge for this meeting. If both parties feel a need and desire to go into the creation of a Financial *Life* Plan, all elements associated with this, including any possible costs, will be discussed. We feel very strongly about full disclosure and complete transparency.

If we move forward with your Financial *Life* Plan, Exhibit 19 summarizes what you can expect from us.

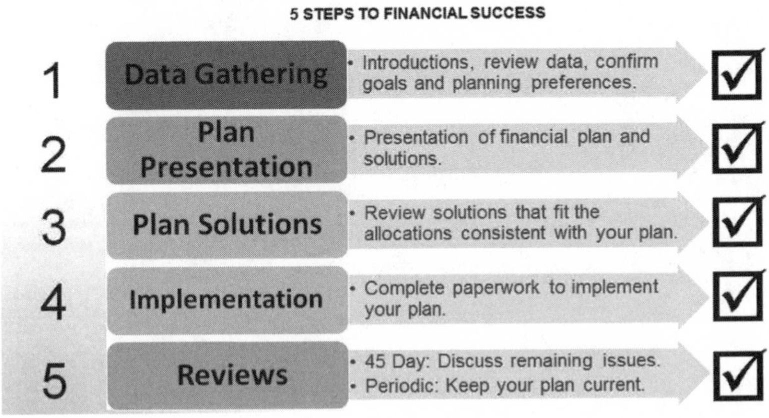

5 STEPS TO FINANCIAL SUCCESS

1	Data Gathering	• Introductions, review data, confirm goals and planning preferences.	☑
2	Plan Presentation	• Presentation of financial plan and solutions.	☑
3	Plan Solutions	• Review solutions that fit the allocations consistent with your plan.	☑
4	Implementation	• Complete paperwork to implement your plan.	☑
5	Reviews	• 45 Day: Discuss remaining issues. • Periodic: Keep your plan current.	☑

Exhibit 19: Steps to Financial Success © RPI

AFTERWORD

I'VE REFERENCED FINANCIAL *LIFE* Planner throughout the book. The word *Life* is italicized as part of our branding at RPI, because we are not just interested in you having enough money to pay your bills and take a couple trips after retirement. We have a burning desire to not only help you through this short-term time of transition, but to also help you live a life full of meaningful purpose that fulfills your ideal compelling vision. Yes, we are interested in making sure you do not pay any unnecessary taxes or penalties and diversify your portfolio in a manner that gives you the highest probability of success without any more risk than necessary. However, we want *more* for you. We want to be part of helping you realize your goals and dreams with your financial resources. To add the *Life* to your Financial *Life* Plan, I have put the Blueprint in the appendix of this book.

I've conducted hundreds of seminars and workshops for Fortune 500 companies and outplacement firms. I want to end this book the same way I end my seminars and workshops, and that's with these two comments:

1. It's good to have money and all the things money can buy. But it's also good to stop every now and then just to check up on ourselves to make sure we don't lose sight of any of the things money can't buy. Your period of transition has you stopped, so perhaps it's the perfect time to do that checkup.

2. People don't plan to fail; they fail to plan. The good news is that you don't have to be one of them! Now that you understand the basics of creating your personal Financial Life Plan and have a trusted resource to provide it, take the first step today and contact us for a Second Opinion. We'll review your current plan or create a new one to help you on your journey to financial success.

> It's always good to get a second opinion.

APPENDIX

PERSONAL BLUEPRINTING

If you were going to take a long trip, you would not just pull out of your driveway and take off; you'd start with a plan that mapped out your destination and the most efficient route. The map for the *Life* part of your Financial *Life* Plan is a Personal Blueprint. Just as you would make sure you took the most efficient route for your trip, your Financial *Life* Plan becomes the basis for your financial decisions, both short- and long-term.

This book focuses on the financial planning aspects of your Financial *Life* Plan. In the appendix, we will focus on the life aspect with a Personal Blueprint. Together, they will form your Financial *Life* Plan. I did my first Blueprint in 2004 and have repeated the process during a holiday vacation from December 27 to January 2 for the new year since. I start out every New Year with my Personal Blueprint and goals in place.

I've had countless newly transitioned people sit across from me either at my desk or through a webcam. Whenever I've asked, "What do you want to do next?" they don't know. The older the person is, the more they are unsure about what they want to do. Shouldn't older, more experienced people have a better idea of what they want to do versus younger, less-experienced ones? I would think yes, but that's not the case. Whether you are looking for the next job or looking for ways to retire, the Personal Blueprint will give you clarity.

Additionally, whenever you are having difficulty making a major decision, I have often found that when I reflect back on my Blueprint, especially the Values area, decisions are easier to make. As an example, I was thinking about buying a plane and becoming a recreational pilot. I went as far as to meet the sales rep that worked for the company whose plane I was interested in and fly in a similar plane to the factory in another state. I was having trouble deciding whether I should make the purchase and start flying lessons, so I turned to my Personal Blueprint. I revisited my values and noted God, health, family (immediate and members of my client family), and friends. I revisited what I consider my meaningful purpose in life to be, and read my compelling vision again. Spending approximately 200 hours away from the things I listed as my top values to become a certified instrument-rated pilot was not in sync with my Personal Blueprint, so I decided against it. Without the Personal Blueprint, I might have spent a lot of money and time on a plane and lessons before realizing it was not a fit.

Also, when you are in a funk and just going through the motions, the Personal Blueprint can help you determine why. The last time I was feeling like this, I revisited my Personal

Blueprint and saw that even though my top values were God, health, and family, I wasn't going to church, working out, or spending quality time with my family. No wonder I was in a funk! After realizing this, I got back into church, the gym, and dates with my wife, and I felt great.

The bottom line is that the Personal Blueprint can change you from living life by default instead of by design.

THE JOURNEY TO FINANCIAL *LIFE* PLANNING

Imagine it's a crisp Saturday morning. The sun is shining, the bags are packed, the seatbelts are fastened, and the car has gas. Everything and everyone is ready. There is only one thing missing: the destination.

Although there was excitement about preparing for this journey, no one ever decided where they really wanted to go. They just knew they wanted to go *somewhere*. Let's apply this logic to job transition and Financial *Life* Planning.

You took a job out of college to pay off some school loans and see if it was going to fulfill you. By the time you paid off your school loans, you figured out the job wasn't a good fit, but you were married, had kids, a mortgage payment, car payments, and a dog. Additionally, you found yourself living in a downsizing world, job-wise, so you spent your time and energy making sure you kept your job. Did you wake up zestfully each morning, looking forward to your day, or did you fall into the following routine?

The alarm goes off and you hit the snooze button. Once you get up, you hit the shower, grab a cup of coffee as you rush out the door without any time for a healthy breakfast, and start your morning commute. You hit the grind all day, often eating lunch at your desk (if you get time to eat at all). Before you know it, it's time to start your commute back home. You walk in exhausted, have a quick meal with your significant other, and spend a few minutes with your kids and tell them goodnight. Soon, you're hitting that snooze button and starting all over again.

Let me share something that you might find hard to believe. I have listened to countless clients over the past thirty years describe their life along these lines. After they tell me how miserable they have been in their current career, I ask, "What would you enjoy doing for your next job?"

Here comes the surprising part. Whether they are thirty, forty, fifty, or sixty, the majority of them give the same answer, "I have no idea."

Isn't it amazing that we can spend decades working and still not know what we want to do? Well that's exactly what this Personal Blueprinting exercise will help you discover. Countless clients of mine have used the Personal Blueprinting tool to figure out what is meaningful to them, so they live each day with purpose. The snooze button never needs to be hit again!

The Personal Blueprinting process is a series of exercises created to help you map out your life. The purpose of these exercises is to help ignite your relentless burning desire and lead you to personal fulfillment. It will help you find your "why." In this series of exercises, you'll develop a clear map of where you want to go personally and what you want to accomplish professionally. This new clarity will make your life more meaningful and your career more successful.

Just like GPS gives you an overview of your directions, here's an overview of the Blueprinting process:

1. Identify your *values*—certain things are important to you. Are you living those values day in, day out?

2. Find your *meaningful purpose* in life—what are you called to do? Will it be remembered after you're gone?

3. Create a *compelling vision* of your future. What is your personal vision of success and significance? What do these accomplishments look like?

4. Develop a *personal mission* statement. Where are you trying to go? How can you make it be easier to get there?

5. Set SMAC-certified *goals* (specific, measurable, achievable, compatible). Wouldn't it be helpful to track your progress along the way?

Now that we have outlined the steps, it's time to get in gear and create a map that can become your go-to guide whenever you need direction.

Step 1: Identify What You Value Most

We all have certain principles and values we believe in and live by. These innermost beliefs distinguish who we are and how we conduct ourselves. Values are things that are very important to us. They include aspects of life such as family, health, career, and spirituality. Having strong convictions about what we value, and keeping them front and center in our lives, keeps us balanced and focused on the things that are most important to us.

In the long run, focusing on what you value, coupled with solid principles, will help you live a life far more satisfying than any short-term gain from compromising. Having strong convictions benefits you in other ways, too. In times of indecision, you can turn to your guiding values. As an example, I thought I wanted to buy a plane and take flying lessons. However, when I compared the time and expense that would have been involved with my values, (God, family, client family, and health) I realized that the plane was not a fit, and my Blueprint helped me decide not to get into flying.

When you're unhappy, you can turn to your values and see if you're leading a life that is consistent with what you value most. The Blueprint can be your life compass. For example, once I was feeling flat, non-energized, and like I was just going through the motions of life. I looked back at my values and realized I had not been going to church, had not been spending enough time with my family, had not been proactively reaching out to my clients, and had stopped working out. No wonder I wasn't feeling energized: I wasn't doing the things I valued the most. I immediately modified my behavior to be more in sync with my values and in no time was feeling re-energized.

Decision-Making

Have you ever had trouble making a decision? In business and in life, we have to make decisions all the time.

Many of them involve gray areas where more than one solution works. These gray areas can lead to indecisiveness, and indecisiveness results when you are not clear on your values. Once you bring clarity to your values, making decisions becomes easy.

Happiness

Far too many people go through life without enthusiasm. Frequently, they are acting in ways that are not congruent with who they are. The result can be burnout, depression, and ineffectiveness. The key is to evaluate what is important to you and then make sure your life is in sync with that.

Achievement

Some of life's greatest fulfillment has come from people who were so dedicated to their values that they were willing to devote their lives to them and to honor them. The key is to feel so strongly about your values you are motivated to take action and live by them. Having conviction about something you value, and then committing to live by it every single day, will go a long way toward igniting your relentless burning desire.

In this exercise, you'll identify what you value most in life and then rank each item from most important to least important. Examples that might appear on your list include the following:

Family   Health   Spiritual

Fulfillment   Love   Relationships   Generosity

Adventure   Achievement   Passion

Creativity   Leaving a Legacy

Fun/Happiness   Positive Attitude

Learning   Helping Others   Simplicity

Financial Security   Peace of Mind

Respect   Gratitude   Abundance

Compassion   Faith   Growth   Honesty   Integrity

Kindness   Selflessness   Significance   Vitality

Wisdom   Intimacy   Security   Peace

DIRECTIONS:

List at least six things you value most in life and rank them in order of importance. Then, indicate the actual percentage of time you spend living and supporting these values.

Things I value most in life are—

Value	Rank	% of Time

Take a close look at your list. Are you spending a lot of time living and supporting your values?

Remember, values are not some fluffy ideal. They are fundamental to who you are. Some of your values may change over time due to changing circumstances in your life. What's important to you today may not be as important to you five years from now. Consequently, it's important to review your values on a regular basis.

To get more focused on your values, restate your top six values in the following chart, then list one key action you can implement that will help you more fully integrate that value into your life. For example, let's say health is one of your top six values. Here's how that line on the chart might look:

Value	Action to integrate it more fully into my life
Health	Exercise at least 30 minutes a day. 5 days a week.

Now complete the full chart:

Value	Action to integrate it more fully into my life

You'll refer to this chart a little later as you work on developing your goals. Review this list on a regular basis to keep your values top of mind.

Step 2: Find Your Meaningful Purpose

To find your meaningful purpose, look beyond the day-to-day pursuits of life to see what truly moves you. What causes you to jump out of bed in the morning, feeling refreshed and ready to tackle the day's challenges? What higher purpose calls you? What is something larger than yourself that inspires you? What can you do that uses all your skills, talents, and interests and benefits the world?

Without meaningful purpose, we simply go through the motions of daily life. We respond to the alarm clock, we go to work, we solve the day's problems, we eat, we relax, we spend a few minutes with the family, we go to bed, and then we wake up and do it all over again. We could do that for fifty years, and then look back on what we've accomplished and be sadly disappointed at how much time we spent accomplishing so little. Each of us is capable of making a very positive impact on the lives of those around us.

For many people, being a loving spouse and raising great kids is a huge accomplishment, and they should be rightfully proud of that. Meaningful purpose goes a step beyond and transcends what we do for ourselves and our immediate family. Meaningful purpose reaches out to the world and infuses other people's lives with the special gifts each of us has.

The following exercise is designed to help you identify, unlock, and pursue your meaningful purpose, so the world can benefit from your unique gifts. Before you answer the following series of questions, reflect on them. Then, write your response and consciously decide how you are going to move forward living your life with meaningful purpose.

1. Are you committed to finding your meaningful purpose, and if so, what has happened in your life that now makes you ready?

2. What are your unique gifts? What do you do extremely well?

3. What do you most value in life? (Restate your top values from Step 1.)

4. What activities are you most passionate about? What gives you a great feeling of satisfaction?

5. What social issues do you care enough about that you would write an editorial in your local newspaper advocating your position?

6. Given a choice, do you prefer to help people by rolling up your sleeves and pitching in, or do you prefer a more behind-the-scenes role? Give examples of the types of activities you like to do based on your response.

7. When you feel empty and directionless in life, what is missing during that time that is causing you to feel that way?

8. How are you nourishing your soul spiritually?

9. Is your spouse or significant other supportive of your desire to live more meaningfully? If not, how are you reconciling that?

10. How do you go about making an important decision about your life direction? Is it made from a surface level, or do you have a way of checking into your soul? Do you have a confidant you can share your thoughts with who can help guide you?

11. Do you view a lack of money as an impediment to fully realizing your purpose? If so, what are some creative ways that you can get past this issue?

12. If you live your life meaningfully, how will the world be a better place?

13. How will you know you are living your life with purpose?

Based on your answers to the previous questions, take some time to jot down your thoughts on what your purpose in life may be. Granted, this is a tall order, but you have to start somewhere. Make some notes, then set these aside for a while and let it sink in. Revisit what you wrote and see if it still feels congruent. Continue this process until you come to the "aha" moment, and you know you've got it!

Meaningful Purpose Notes

Step 3: Create a Compelling Vision of Your Future

There's an old saying, "If you don't know where you're going, any road will get you there." That's a recipe for mediocrity. People who have great achievements know exactly where they're going, and they take the necessary steps to get there. But, where is "there" for you?

"There" is your ideal future scenario. It is the dream life and business you would create if you had absolutely no constraints. It's your vision for your surroundings, the people you associate with, what you spend your time doing, and what you want to accomplish. It's different for everybody. For example, perhaps you want to be successfully self-employed, working from home, and living in the mountains. Or, perhaps you want to work for a nonprofit organization that speaks to your heart and live near your children and grandchildren. It can be anything, but it must be clearly defined. It must include tangibles, so you can see it, feel it, touch it, smell it, and hear it.

Your vision must be compelling. It must be something that motivates you to jump out of bed in the morning and get moving. Your vision is what will sustain you when the going gets tough and you face major obstacles. To develop it, disengage from the present and position yourself in a future with unlimited possibilities. Eliminate your limiting beliefs and think big. With this frame of mind, you can develop a vision that propels you to success, contribution, and happiness beyond what you've ever imagined.

The key to your compelling vision is to create one that motivates you to take action and helps you persevere. Here's an example of a compelling vision of the future:

"I enthusiastically jump out of bed every morning full of love for God, family, friends, and life. I am a husband my wife is proud of, a father my children look up to, and a friend people count on.

My family is financially secure, physically fit, and emotionally close. We live in a comfortable home on one acre with a postcard-perfect view of open water. Our home is light and airy, with crisp ocean breezes blowing through. Pictures of my family and special moments in our life line the walls. The sound of grandchildren fills the house.

My days are spent helping the people around me reach their fullest potential. I do this by meeting with my top clients, guiding them in reaching their dreams and aspirations, and communicating my wisdom through my life planning website. My financial success enables me to be a reverse tither, and I give away 90% of my income and live on 10%. My schedule is flexible, and I spend several hours a week mentoring disadvantaged children. For recreation, my wife and I travel the world, visit our kids and grandkids, read, and take time to enjoy the beauty of the great outdoors.

When I go to bed at night, I sleep soundly knowing I helped make the world a little better than it was when I woke up."

DIRECTIONS

In this next exercise, you will paint a picture of your compelling vision. Don't hold back. Finish each statement as accurately and completely as possible. This is your future, so make it a great one!

1. My ideal working environment is . . .

2. The relationships I want to surround myself with include . . .

3. I want to spend my days working on . . .

4. If I weren't so afraid, I would . . .

5. My life will not be complete unless I . . .

    a. If I knew for certain I would die peacefully in either 14 days or 14 weeks (and I didn't know which of these two dates I would die), I would do the following in the next 14 days . . .

    b. And, I would do the following in the remaining 12 weeks (assuming I live that long). .

6. If I had all the money I ever needed, I would spend the rest of my life . . .

7. I want people to remember me by saying I was . . .

8. My most memorable experiences include . . .

9. The part of my weekly routine I look forward to is . . .

10. I feel alive and energetic after I have just . . .

11. The community or world issue I feel most strongly about is . . .

12. It may seem impossible today, but my life would dramatically improve if . . .

Review how you finished the previous statements. From this, use the following outline to write a compelling vision that excites you and motivates you to take action. Remember to include who you'd like to surround yourself with, where you'd like to live, how you'd like to spend your days, and what you'd like to accomplish.

Once you create a vision that gives you goose bumps, review it daily to hardwire it into your life so it will keep inspiring you.

My compelling vision is to . . .

_____

_____

_____

_____

_____

_____

_____

_____

_____

_____

_____

Step 4: Develop a Personal and Professional Mission Statement

A mission statement is not simply a hokey phrase that gets written once and then filed away. Rather, it is a living, breathing document. You should prominently display it for reinforcement and to internalize its message. Spend time developing, memorizing, and living your mission statement and you'll be pleasantly surprised by the results.

Personal Mission Statement

Creating a personal mission statement will be one of the most important things you do. Set aside some time to reflect and complete it. Your personal mission statement will evolve over time, but it is important to get a draft on paper, so you can continue to shape it.

A personal mission statement is a bold statement about the kind of life you want to lead, the kind of person you want to be, and how you want to conduct yourself. It will serve as your lighthouse during difficult times and keep you motivated and focused during your life. Share it with your spouse or significant other.

Here's an example of a personal mission statement:

"My mission is to be loving and loyal to my family and friends, lead a successful career I enjoy, stay healthy, and take on challenges that come my way. I value my family, friends, spiritual fulfillment, sense of accomplishment, and enthusiasm. I value my relationship with God and live by the Golden Rule.

Throughout my life, I will always be supportive and loyal to my family, clients, and friends. I will be an active member in my place of worship and in my local community. I will use my financial management skills to help needy organizations keep their financial houses in order. I will live life to the fullest and strongly believe that nothing is impossible."

Your personal mission statement may follow a similar format or you may want to modify it. The key is to make it personal, meaningful, and inspirational.

DIRECTIONS

In this exercise, you'll create your personal mission statement. A personal mission statement is your declaration of the kind of person you want to be. It answers questions such as who do I want to be? How do I conduct myself? What and who are important to me? Think of it as a daily guide to living.

Take some time to draft your personal mission statement. The key is to get something down on paper. Let it percolate and then come back to it. Eventually, solidify and review it each day.

Personal Mission Statement

_____

_____

_____

_____

_____

_____

_____

_____

_____

_____

_____

_____

_____

_____

_____

_____

_____

Professional Mission Statement

Your professional mission statement is your business guide. It can address issues such as who you are, why you exist, whom you serve, and what results your clients can expect. After you develop it, share it with your significant other or friends. Let it permeate your home and guide your actions.

Here are several examples of professional mission statements submitted by financial advisors:

"To create a world of financial comfort by implementing custom solutions to individual needs!"

"We are dedicated to enhancing the quality of our clients' lives as we oversee their wealth to help them achieve their long-term goals and dreams. With our unmatched, superior service and guidance, we build strong relationships as we help simplify our clients' financial affairs, allowing them to focus on those areas that give their life meaning and purpose."

"To guide our clients through the process of obtaining financial peace of mind so they can focus on the most important things in life."

"To guide our clients in making wise decisions based on Biblical principles for wealth management."

Make your professional mission statement personal, meaningful, and inspirational, like you did with your personal mission statement. Both statements should be reasonably short and highly memorable. There's no set length to a mission statement. Just make sure you can remember it and that it connects with you.

DIRECTIONS

In this exercise, you'll create your professional mission statement. A professional mission statement is your declaration of the kind of business or career you want to have. It answers questions such as: What does my firm do? How do we do it? Why do we exist? What can our clients expect? If you are an employee and not a business owner, write it from the perspective of how you do your job.

Take some time to draft your professional mission statement. You just want to get something down on paper. Meditate and then come back to it. Eventually, solidify and review it each day.

Professional Mission Statement

_____

_____

_____

_____

_____

_____

_____

_____

_____

_____

_____

_____

_____

Step 5: Express Your Value

A value proposition defines what makes your practice unique and what experience you want your clients to have. A simple way to create a value proposition is to select keywords from your professional mission statement and define its keywords. Try to answer why a prospect should do business with you or what your client's ideal experience should be.

DIRECTIONS

Evaluate the draft you created of your professional mission statement. It should be one sentence long and address the following questions:

1. Who are you and what makes you different?

2. What do you actually do for your clients?

3. How do you do it?

Professional Mission Statement

See previous section and rewrite your professional mission statement here.

_____

_____

_____

_____

_____

_____

SAMPLE VALUE PROPOSITION FROM A FINANCIAL LIFE PLANNING FIRM:

You are here today to decide if there is a compelling reason for you to work with me and my practice.

Our mission is to inspire our clients in making informed decisions through education, communication, and service that exceeds their expectations.

Our mission statement is more than just words; it's the action we take. Let me define for you what a few of the keywords in our mission statement mean to me.

Inspire

Our goal is to inspire you, our client, to live your life by design, not by default. Money is a tool to get the most out of your life.

Informed Decisions

Once you are inspired to share what you want out of life, next, we help you make informed decisions that are logical for you. Our skilled financial planners and other specialist bring our resources together to develop a plan, so you can accomplish your dreams.

Education

You can only make informed decisions if we educate you. You don't need to understand everything we are doing, but you do need an aerial view of what we are doing, why we are doing it, and how it applies to you.

Communication

Our communication doesn't stop at education. Many firms claim to communicate frequently with clients, but we take it a step further and we over communicate, so you know we think of you as a person and not just an account. You will never be disappointed in the level of communication you receive from us.

Service that Exceeds Your Expectations

We deliver a level of service that will exceed your expectations. In our country, expectation of service has never been lower. So, we are going in a different direction. We provide a Four Seasons experience with Southwest Airlines efficiency.

How can we do all this? We are independent and sit on the same side of the table as you. We have a seamless proactive service process; we anticipate your needs before you even know you have them. It means being bifocal, which means paying attention to what is happening today and anticipating changes on the horizon. Additionally, the entire team does their piece to add value to the process, which means it's not about working with David Blaydes but about having a systemized approach so you get to experience the firm way.

Create your Value Proposition

After you have a solid mission statement, you can create your value proposition. In your professional mission statement, highlight three to five keywords you can define for your clients and prospects to answer the following questions:

1. Why should I do business with you?

2. What will my experience be like working with you?

Keyword or Phrase #1: _____
Define: _____

Keyword or Phrase #2: _____
Define: _____

Keyword or Phrase #3: _____
Define: _____

Keyword or Phrase #4: _____
Define: _____

Keyword or Phrase #5: _____
Define: _____

PUT IT ALL TOGETHER!

Create a story by drawing together your keywords from your mission statement and ending with a punch line. Connect it all together (e.g., see the sample value proposition we shared earlier).

Your Value Proposition

_____

_____

_____

_____

_____

_____

_____

_____

_____

_____

_____

_____

_____

_____

_____

_____

_____

_____

Step 6: Set 1-, 3-, 5-, and 10-Year Goals

We all have wants and desires. We all daydream about what it would be like to be living our ideal lives. Unfortunately, merely thinking about our ideal lives will not get us there. We have to be clear about what we want, when we want it, and why we want it, and we have to take positive action to make it happen. The goal-setting process is crucial to making all this happen. As we set goals, make sure they are SMAC-certified—specific, measurable, achievable, and compatible.

One of the keys to setting your goals is to tie them into your compelling vision. Your compelling vision is a lifetime pursuit. To make that manageable, you have to break it into pieces. To do this, complete the goal-setting and action-planning exercises. Start by reviewing your compelling vision and then work backward to set your goals. To pursue your vision, what has to happen in ten years, five years, three years, and one year? Determine what ages you, your spouse, and your children will be at each of those time periods. Identify the goal and then determine the one activity that will have the greatest impact on reaching that goal. Also, identify the reward you will get from reaching the goal.

Here are examples of categories in which you might want to set goals:

- Attitude—are there any attitudes or limiting beliefs you need to change to reach your compelling vision?

- Career—what do you want to accomplish in your professional life?

- Education—do you need additional knowledge to pursue your vision?

- Family—how can you improve your relationships?

- Financial—what net worth are you striving for? What business financial goals do you have?

- Physical—what specific physical goals can you set? Do you want to be a certain weight? Do you want to exercise a certain amount? Is there a challenging physical goal you'd like to achieve, such as climbing Mount Rainier?

- Recreation—what do you want to do in your free time that will rejuvenate you?

- Community—what do you want to do for your community? What legacy do you want to leave?

- Spiritual—how do you want to grow in your spirituality?

Once you've set your goals, transfer them to the Visualize and Realize section. This will neatly summarize your compelling vision and all the activities that have to take place to make it happen.

Sample One-Year Goals

Goal	Key Activity to Achieve	Reward
Change my belief system from scarcity to abundance	Read the appropriate books, listen to the right speakers, and take them to heart	A better outlook on life
Take a two-week family vacation	Schedule it	Grow closer as a family, smiling faces, new experiences
Exercise vigorously at least 5 days per week	Join the local health club, get up by 5:15 a.m., and hire a personal trainer for 6 months	Great health, feel good, more energy
Break 80 in golf	More practice and focus on eliminating double bogies	New set of clubs
Become a member of the leadership team at my place of work	Express my desire and follow the protocol to obtain the position	Being able to help people
Meditate at least 15 minutes a day	Find a consistent time that works and create a peaceful space	Stress reduction, clear mind, greater understanding
Spend 5 hours per week helping kids with homework or as much time as needed	Let kids know I'm available and make it a priority	Smarter, happier kids, satisfaction from helping, grow closer to the kids

DIRECTIONS

On the following pages, write down your goals for the next one-, three-, five-, and ten-year periods. After that, transfer the goals that relate to you achieving your compelling vision.

1-Year Goals

MY AGE:	SPOUSE'S AGE:	KID'S AGE:

Goal	Key Activity to Achieve	Reward

3-Year Goals

MY AGE:	SPOUSE'S AGE:	KID'S AGE:

Goal ·	Key Activity to Achieve	Reward

5-Year Goals

MY AGE:	SPOUSE'S AGE:	KID'S AGE:

Goal	Key Activity to Achieve	Reward

10-Year Goals

MY AGE:	SPOUSE'S AGE:	KID'S AGE:

Goal	Key Activity to Achieve	Reward

Visualize and Realize

Year 1 Goals

Year 3 Goals

Year 5 Goals

Year 10 Goals

ABOUT THE AUTHOR

DAVID L. BLAYDES, MS, CFP®, RFC®, AIF®, is the founder and CEO of Retirement Planners International, Inc., (RPI) and has been successfully engaged in the financial planning industry since 1977. His background and experience eminently qualify him in offering comprehensive Financial *Life* Planning to help fulfill the needs of individuals faced with financial decisions, as he has specialized in job transition planning through companies and outplacement firms for over twenty-five years. Mr. Blaydes also donates financial plans through a local charity for those with cancer.

Mr. Blaydes has a bachelor's degree in business and a master's degree in financial planning and has been a member of the International Association for Financial Planning (IAFP) since 1986. He received his Certified Financial Planner (CFP®) in 1987. (He is also a Registered Financial Consultant (RFC) and an Accredited Investment Fiduciary (AIF®).

In addition, Mr. Blaydes has appeared on the *NBC Nightly News* with Tom Brokaw, TLN's *Money IQ*, and *Significant Insights*. He has also appeared on *Smart Money*, Boomer Financial

Radio Network, and was a cohost of *America's Wealth Management National* radio show. His insights have also appeared in Crain's *Chicago Business, Financial Planning Magazine, Investment News, Financial Advisor, Chicago Sun Times, Daily Herald, Naperville Sun,* and others.

In 2012, Mr. Blaydes was nationally recognized as a finalist for the prestigious *Investment News* Volunteer of the Year award for his volunteer work helping those with cancer with their Financial *Life* Planning. In 2013, he was named *Financial Planning Magazine's* Planner of the Year for his pro bono work with cancer patients and was on the cover of their August 2013 issue.

Mr. Blaydes has worked with many Fortune 500 companies during periods of downsizing and has assisted outplacement firms on a national basis for 25 years. He uses his experience, education, and credentials to guide people through a stressful financial and emotional time while offering both financial survival strategies and emotional reassurances.